The Two-Year College Instructor Today

Arthur M. Cohen
Florence B. Brawer

The Praeger Special Studies program, through a selective worldwide distribution network, makes available to the academic, government, and business communities significant and timely research in U.S. and international economic, social, and political issues.

The Two-Year College Instructor Today

PRAEGER SPECIAL STUDIES IN U.S. ECONOMIC, SOCIAL, AND POLITICAL ISSUES

Praeger Publishers   New York   London

83873

Library of Congress Cataloging in Publication Data

Cohen, Arthur M
    The two-year college instructor today.

    (Praeger special studies in U.S. economic, social,
and political issues)
    Bibliography: p.
    Includes index.
    1. College teachers—United States. 2. Junior
colleges—United States. I. Brawer, Florence B.,
1922–   joint author. II. Title.
LB2331.7.C62   378.1'2'0973   77–83482
ISBN 0-03-039706-5

Portions of this book were provided by the
ERIC Clearinghouse for Junior Colleges.

PRAEGER SPECIAL STUDIES
200 Park Avenue, New York, N.Y., 10017, U.S.A.

Published in the United States of America in 1977
by Praeger Publishers,
A Division of Holt, Rinehart and Winston, CBS, Inc.

789   038   987654321

This book is lovingly dedicated to our mothers,
Rae Berke Cohen and Sali Wintner Blum

ACKNOWLEDGMENTS

No long-sustaining project is ever conducted in a vacuum. In the case of this book and the research on which it is based, many people were involved to whom we owe appreciation. We are especially grateful to Stanley Turesky, our project director from the Office of Planning and Analysis, National Endowment for the Humanities. His interest in the study from its inception, his watchful eye through its every phase, and his astute criticisms all contributed to the project's success.

Leslie Koltai, chancellor of the Los Angeles Community College District, also has been involved throughout. As a former member of the National Council on the Humanities, he was instrumental in alerting the endowment to the need to attend to the two-year colleges in America. His concern and guidance were of inestimable value.

Sue Schlesinger, administrative coordinator of the Center for the Study of Community Colleges, worked on all aspects of the project in a number of capacities. Her willingness and faithfulness helped to make it the interesting venture it has been.

Others were involved, and we gratefully acknowledge their help: Bonnie Sanchez, associate director of the Educational Resources Information Center (ERIC) Clearinghouse for Junior Colleges at the University of California at Los Angeles, who was always ready to provide a reference or find needed information; the graduate students who participated in our spring 1976 seminar at UCLA; Victor Cruz-Cardona, who provided valuable insights to the study; and Milton Rokeach who graciously allowed us to use his Terminal Values Survey once again. Eleanor Murray and Chris Christian of Field Research Corporation in San Francisco printed the Faculty Survey, tabulated the data, and relieved us of considerable headaches.

Participants in our Humanities Conference and in our seminars in Los Angeles, Chicago, and Washington, D.C., were also helpful in a number of ways—offering suggestions for the humanities, presenting ways in which they would be enhanced, and responding to our many inquiries. Their concern and interest in this area of study bodes well for the disciplines concerned.

We also gratefully acknowledge the help of the presidents and facilitators of the 156 colleges who had the commitment and professionalism to participate in this project; the colleges involved in the pilot study; and the many faculty members and chairpersons who responded to our survey. Without their help—much of it time consuming—there would have been no project to report. And finally, we thank the National Endowment for the Humanities for their support. To these many people, our thanks and appreciation.

CONTENTS

LIST OF TABLES

INTRODUCTION

At the core of every school—from kindergarten through the graduate institution—lies the faculty. Except for the students' peers, these are the people with whom students have the most contact and the figures who command the most authority, by virtue of their positions if not their actual personage. And although they may lament their own impotency in institutional governance, they exercise powerful positions within their own domain.

Although faculty were typically slighted earlier in written reports about academia (researchers and writers apparently found college presidents and students far more interesting), more recently they have drawn their own share of attention. There are many books now about college teachers, and some of them include data about two-year colleges. A few books are concerned with two-year college instructors exclusively. The faculty in two-year junior or community colleges have been addressed by Garrison (1967), Kelley and Wilbur (1970), and O'Banion (1973), as well as in our own work: Brawer (1968), Cohen (1973), and Cohen and Brawer (1969; 1972). Little by little, the faculty members—so important to a college's functioning—are being recognized in the literature. Their strengths and weaknesses are noted, orientation to work cited, and functioning as mature professionals described.

Much is known about some aspects of the faculty, little about others. This is not surprising because there are no longitudinal data bases on which a researcher might draw. Most reported studies are one-shot affairs: a dissertation or thesis written by a graduate student; a compilation drawn together by a professional association; a report from a local or state education agency. Each investigator asks his own questions, prepares a unique survey instrument, and defines the sample population in his own way. Data have been compiled, but little attention has been given to comparability or to the amalgamation of representative profiles.

Nonetheless, reasonably consistent profiles may be drawn on certain characteristics of the two-year college faculty. We know what degrees they have and where they were trained. In the early 1970s the figures on highest degree held showed 3 to 10 percent with the doctorate; 65 to 80 percent, masters; 14 to 27 percent, bachelors. (The lower figures for doctorates and masters pertained when all faculty—occupational and academic, full-time and part-time—were viewed together.) The majority of those involved in teaching college-parallel courses were prepared in traditional masters programs at senior institutions. Teachers in occupational programs had experience in the trade. The Masters of Arts in Teaching or Master of Arts in College Teaching programs were not widely utilized by community college personnel.

We know where the faculty come from. Many of them previously taught in the lower schools;Medsker and Tillery (1971) reported that one-third of the faculty had prior public school experience. But Phair's data show the percent of newly employed California instructors with secondary school experience dropping steadily, from 36 percent in 1967 to 15 percent in 1974. Some—an increasing number—had prior experience in four-year institutions.

Some information on professional functioning is also available. Collected reports reveal that these instructors tend not to write or to conduct research. Compared with their counterparts in other types of colleges, they tend not to participate in professional or scholarly associations. Their emphasis is on teaching. The average number of class hours taught by each full-time instructor in the two-year college is down from the 15 to 17 hours per week reported in studies done in the early 1970s; by 1975 it was between 13 and 15 hours. But few studies are available on what else faculty do during their work week, and even fewer on the involvement of part-time instructors.

Comparisons between part-time and full-time faculty in terms of preparation, experience, and teaching styles have been notably lacking, although some statewide studies have been done recently in North Carolina and California. This topic is significant because the part-time instructor is now represented in the community colleges at an increasing rate; in fall 1975, in all two-year colleges, there were more part-time faculty than full-timers. Typically, they enjoy fewer perquisites, much less job security, and lower salaries and fringe benefits.

The information about faculty satisfaction, aspirations, and values is scattered. Much of it was compiled and presented in the Center for the Study of Community Colleges, *The Faculty in Review* (1975). More is contained in this book. This information is more difficult to gather than are the demographic data, although it is at least as interesting and potentially more useful. We know, for example, that a high percentage of two-year college faculty members would prefer to teach in four-year colleges for reasons of increased status and a lighter teaching load (Medsker and Tillery found 44 percent saying they would prefer university positions); but, as two-year college teaching tends to become more a career in its own right, these figures may be reduced.

Collectively the faculty exhibits a picture of an occupational grouping in a nascent stage of professionalization. Its characterization as a profession is exemplified by the requirement of a long period of training before one can practice within it, the formation of professional associations, and the view held by outsiders and by those who practice within it. Its shortcomings as a profession are seen in its failure to control entry into and to police its own ranks, and its lack of adherence to a body of specialized knowledge not readily available to laymen. Further, it has developed neither a unique ethos nor a code of ethics to which its members subscribe.

This book is about the faculty both as individuals and as a functioning professional body. As the faculty have grown in number—by 1976 there were nearly 200,000 of them—they have gained in stature and visibility, leading to their being studied in their own right rather than merely as an adjunct to studies of faculty in all higher education. Source material for the book has been gathered from numerous studies of instructors in two-year institutions, particularly from a study conducted in 1975 by the Center for the Study of Community Colleges acting under the sponsorship of the National Endowment for the Humanities, a federal agency established by Congress to support research, education, and public activities in the humanities.

This book includes information useful to instructors who wish to understand more about their colleagues across the country, to coordinators of faculty preparation programs and in-service faculty development activities, to those who would make policy affecting the faculty, and to students of the community college as an institution. All can learn of faculty perceptions, attitudes, and orientation toward the various aspects of their work.

Information about all aspects of faculty life is contained in the text. The first two chapters relate the current status of the profession and describe the Faculty Survey. The next three chapters focus on the instructor as a person—his attitudes and values, the level of satisfaction with his work, and the level of "functional potential" (a construct built on psychodynamic principles of human functioning). The role of the instructor is detailed in Chapters 6 to 9—orientation toward curriculum and instruction, concern for students, research orientation, and differences between full-time and part-time instructors. Chapter 10 is concerned with faculty development and preparation. It is followed by a chapter on the doctorate, including comparisons of doctorate holder with those who do not have this degree. Chapters 12 and 13 discuss perceptions of the university as a reference point and cite concern with humanities. The final two chapters summarize the most significant findings of the Faculty Survey, offer an interpretation of the faculty as a professional group, and make recommendations for modifications in faculty selection, preparation, and working environment. Those chapters are geared to the two-year colleges and their instructors today—and to their future.

The Two-Year College Instructor Today

THE STATE OF
THE PROFESSION

Numerous pressures changed community colleges more in the early 1970s than in any other comparable period of their history. Different types of students, new statements of mission, varied demands for community services—all had their effect. In response, the colleges shifted not only their curriculums but also many of their basic organizational forms. They tended to broaden their service areas, moving beyond the academic or college-parallel offerings with which they started at the turn of the century and beyond the occupational programs that they instituted in the 1920s and 1930s. They began characterizing themselves as community development centers.

In recounting the forces that moved the colleges, new types of students must be placed at the head of the list. This change can be stated no more dramatically than to report that the median student age nationwide rose from approximately 21 in 1970 to 28 in 1975. Coupled with this shift is an increase in the number of part-time students who, by 1975, outnumbered full-time students by more than 10 percent. The large number of older, part-time students are both the cause and effect of changes in types of programs and curriculums. The students effect changes in curriculum somewhat by their articulated demands but more often by their enrolling in certain types of courses and programs while shunning others. They are interested in a wider range of programs than previously considered—recreational, renewal, retraining. The colleges are offering more career programs. Most of the degree-credit curricular expansion in recent years has been in the allied health and business career fields. The colleges present entry-level programs for people wanting to join those occupational areas, and they offer retraining courses for people already in the fields. The expansion in these areas has been such that more than half the new faculty employed in the 19-state North Central region in 1973 were in allied health, vocational-technical, or business-data processing areas (Brown, 1975). And new faculty employed in

California show a similar pattern, with health services and business fields dominating the employment lists throughout the first half of the decade.

Shifts in college organization have occurred, typified by the development of colleges without walls. The most notable are the Community College of Vermont, founded in 1971, and Whatcom Community College, organized in Washington in 1970. Neither college has a campus nor any full-time faculty members; both offer courses of current interest in numerous locations around the state. More recently, Coastline Community College and the Peralta College for Non-Traditional Study in California, and Pioneer Community College in Missouri, have been organized within multicampus districts as a way of co-ordinating a variety of educational services apart from those offered on existing campuses. Still other colleges wihout walls have been opened or are planned, many not even carrying the appelation, "college;" namely, the Chicago City-Wide Institute and the New Dimension of the Los Angeles Community College District.

Many of the new curricular and organizational patterns are associated with the move toward what has been called "community-based" education, which, regardless of its merit, changes perceptions. As the colleges expand into other than traditional academic and occupational program areas and as they move away from their historic campuses, they extend an evermore diffuse image. Few people within or outside the institutions know what to make of them as their services form and reform. The radical critics who say that the community colleges are antagonistic to the poor because they condemn the underprivileged to a lifetime of low-status jobs have not yet begun to deal with the community college as an agency of direct community involvement. As the institution moves into areas previously served by social welfare agencies, jurisdictional disputes arise. The changes have acted to edge the colleges out of the academic mainstream reaching from kindergarten to the doctorate, and no one is sure how they will fare in uncharted waters. Perhaps the two-year college's fate is to be bombarded with shifting ideas and activities. But it does make it difficult for the people who work there to maintain a practical view of what the institution is about.

The colleges' responses to the various pressures have affected the faculty. The low growth in full-time staffing, the introduction of paraprofessional aides, changed forms of inservice training, the advent of collective bargaining and affirmative action, and the definition of new roles for instructors who choose to conduct their work differently without moving out of the faculty ranks—all these play a part. Even though the jurisdictional disputes between community colleges and other educational service agencies occur at legislative, board, and administrative levels, the instructors are touched. Many began work in one kind of an institution, which rapidly became something else. Further, the new patterns of organization and service have had a major impact on faculty employment practices, working environments, role, and relationships with the institution.

The teaching profession in two-year colleges is marked by many changes. The widespread employment of part-time instructors, which accelerated so that by 1974 there were more part-timers than full-timers in the colleges, has affected professionalization. But because part-timers traditionally have not shared the same benefits and pro-rata pay as full-timers, and because they are not closely affiliated with the full-time activities of the campus, it is difficult for them to be an active part of the profession. Separate organizations comprised of part-time instructors clamoring for equal status and pay change professional outlook and image. Roles are affected when faculty are encouraged to move out of their classrooms and become coordinators of nontraditional programs, or media developers and learning laboratory managers, on the campuses. The change in the client population with whom the staff interacts has a distinct effect on working conditions—teaching adult learners is different from meeting recent high school graduates. These changes are certainly more influential than the trend toward collective bargaining and the demands for affirmative action, both of which have received considerably more attention in the literature about faculty.

It is worth noting also some of the potential effects on the profession that seemed imminent in the early 1970s, but that never materialized. Faculty accountability is first. Many states tried to mandate faculty accountability by modifying faculty evaluation and development processes. Under the prodding of legislatures and state and local governing boards, administrators and instructors were to develop ways of assisting instructors to become accountable for their activities. Should an instructor be assessed and found wanting, he was to be either assisted to improve or, failing that, to be severed from the institution.

A flurry of activity resulted. Some states abolished tenure in favor of a system of continuing contracts. Others mandated elaborate evaluation schemes whereby instructors were to be judged by their students, administrators, peers, and by themselves. College districts developed detailed evaluation guidelines replete with checkpoints, feedback loops, committee structures, and numerous other devices through which instructor evaluation was to occur. The process of developing these guidelines caused consternation among skittish faculty members and proved to be one of the factors accelerating the faculty union movement.

However, faculty evaluation remains of little effect. In most cases where an instructor was identified as wanting, and where he chose to pursue the matter of his severance in the courts, rulings went in his favor. Curiously, despite the elaborate evaluation schemes, the rulings usually turned on the procedures involved; that is, courts frequently found that the instructor was denied due process because he was not informed of the grievance, because the institution did not demonstrate that it had taken all efforts to upgrade his skills, or because it could not prove that the person was deficient in an essential teaching area. In short, the burden of proof remains with the college, and faculty dismissal remains as difficult as it ever was.

Reduction in force was another event forecast but not materialized. In 1970 and 1971 growth in enrollments and in fiscal appropriations slowed. Accordingly, presidents began talking of staff reduction and the question of priority ordering for instructor dismissal came to the fore. Reduction in force, a term that refers to policies and procedures used when dismissal of tenured instructors is made necessary by inadequate finances or discontinuance of an area of instruction, was openly discussed. Staff reductions took place or were contemplated in nearly half of all two-year colleges (Sprenger and Schultz, 1974). Again, many instructors feared their jobs were on the line.

Implementation of reduction in force policies, however, was averted in most institutions because enrollments turned back up in 1973 and because many administrators effected plans for dealing with the potential problems of overstaffing by using the expedient of employing part-time instructors any time a vacancy occurred. In short, in the early 1970s, many colleges simply stopped employing full-time instructors who, by virtue of contractual obligations, enjoyed either tenure or other rights to continued employment. Each time a full-timer left for any reason, he was replaced with one or more part-timers. Through the early 1970s, few part-timers enjoyed the privileges of continual service; most were employed on a semester-by-semester basis. Most pertinent for the profession, even in those areas where reduction in force did take place, the move did not strengthen the faculty by eliminating weak instructors. In almost all cases the procedure was based on time-honored—and court-approved—rules of seniority.

Affirmative action guidelines and rules also promised to affect the faculty. Under Federal Executive Order 11246, institutions were directed to demonstrate that no discrimination existed in any aspect of employment and, further, that affirmative action was being taken to remedy the effects of past discrimination. The composition of the faculty along lines of ethnicity and sex was to be brought into accord with the distribution of women and members of ethnic minorities in the population.

The community colleges did not have as far to go in employing relative numbers of women as did the universities. Whereas the proportion of males to females in university professorial positions is at least three to one, in the community colleges a ratio of approximately two to one pertained. Further, the disproportion of men over women in the universities increases markedly in the higher ranks of the professorship. But in community colleges, where academic ranking tends less to differentiate among the staff than do years of service and commensurate pay, the differences between men and women were less pronounced. In 1975, in all two-year colleges, women averaged $14,501 and men, $16,120 (AACJC, 1975a).

Based on employment figures for new community college faculty, the colleges have made some effort to bring their male-female ratios closer in line. In California, a state with a mature and large community college system, during the early 1970s the ratio of newly employed faculty hovered around 58 percent males, 42 percent females. A similar ratio pertained in the 19-state North Central region, where 1973 employment figures showed 57 percent males gaining new positions in community colleges (Brown, 1975). And, as discerned in our Center for the Study of Community Colleges' 1975 Faculty Survey, the total faculty ratio in a representative sample of colleges organized since 1970 showed the male-female distribution to be 56 percent to 44 percent (even though in colleges organized 15 or more years ago, the ratio was 72 percent to 28 percent). If these tendencies hold, and if the female faculty members stay on the job as long as the males, the current ratio of two to one males over females will tend toward parity.

The two-year colleges' record in employing members of ethnic minorities is not as pronounced. The Faculty Survey found 91 percent Caucasians, 2.6 percent blacks, 0.9 percent Asians, and 1.9 percent Chicanos, figures that closely parallel those reported in the 1971 Project Focus study (Bushnell, 1973) and the 1972 American Council on Education (ACE) survey (Bayer, 1973). The attempts to change the ratios show some promise; but, in the 19-state North Central region, 96 percent of the faculty employed in 1973 were Caucasians. New hires in California during the 1970s showed approximately 8 percent blacks, 9 percent Chicanos, 3 percent Asian-Americans (Phair, 1972; 1974; 1975). The disturbing characteristic is that affirmative action came along at a time when employment of new full-time staff members was down severely. Hence, although a college might have desired to increase its percentage of women and minority group faculty members, its latitude for action was not nearly so great as it was during the 1960s, when staffing was occurring at a much more vigorous pace.

Further, despite all the rhetoric about affirmative action, attitudes among community college staff members show a strong bias against giving preferential treatment to members of minority groups. The 1971 Project Focus survey of community colleges found the goal, "Attract representative numbers of minority faculty members," ranked 24th on a list of 26 "preferred goals" by the presidents, and 11th of 12 by the faculty (Bushnell, 1973). When the two-year college respondents to the 1972 ACE faculty survey were asked whether they think "There should be preferential hiring for women faculty at this institution," 67 percent replied in the negative; 63 percent were opposed to preferential hiring of members of minority groups. The Center for the Study of Community Colleges' Faculty Survey combined preferential hiring of women and ethnic minorities into one query and found 60 percent of the respondents opposed and an additional 16 percent with no opinion. It seems safe to say that a groundswell of favored treatment for minorities has not developed.

Nonetheless, the opportunity to redress the imbalance in faculty ethnic and sex composition in the 1970s was greater in the community colleges than in other types of institutions because the rate of growth had not slowed quite as much. According to the *College and University Bulletin* (AAHE, 1975) available administrative and faculty positions at public two-year colleges had increased from 8 percent of the total listings in 1974 to 26 percent. Whether this presages greater adherence to affirmative actions mandates, it, at least, allows it.

Collective bargaining expanded so rapidly in the community colleges in the early 1970s that it seemed historically inescapable. In 1972–73, public two-year colleges in 16 states and the District of Columbia were operating under collective bargaining agreements. By 1974–75, the number had expanded to 21 states. Of the 904 two-year colleges operating in 1972–73, some 194 had faculty bargaining units that had negotiated for contracts. By 1974–75, of the 975 institutions then existent, 224 had collective bargaining agreements.

The differences between the major bargaining representatives were few and diminishing. Nevertheless, it is instructive to observe that the American Association of University Professors (AAUP), the old-line professional association for higher education faculty, was named as the bargaining unit in only two of the 224 contracts. A combination of the AAUP with the National Education Association was the bargaining agent in seven contracts. The American Federation of Teachers (AFT) held 66 contracts, the National Education Association (NEA), 100 contracts, and a combination of NEA and AFT had 24 contracts. Independent units accounted for the other 25.

Regardless of the bargaining representative, the contracts achieved have a common characteristic—they are all exceedingly detailed, listing and defining rights of the bargaining unit, grievance procedures, hours that may be assigned to instructors, class size, faculty responsibilities, professional development activities, and more. These contracts have been examined by numerous researchers including Lombardi (1975) and Benewitz (1973). In fact, a National Center for the Study of Collective Bargaining in Higher Education has been established and is operating in New York.

Strong positions have been taken by people on both sides of the arguments regarding the pros and cons of collective bargaining. Those who feel it is a necessary idea long overdue say that the faculty role and dedication to responsibility will be greatly enhanced as professors are protected by contracts that limit the extent of administrator interference with their activities and that assure them a living wage. The opposite viewpoint is that collective bargaining will be destructive both to the relationships between faculty and students and the governance structure of the institution because it will move ultimate authority from lay governing boards to an employee agency. Both extreme positions are short of documentation as most commentators have devoted themselves more to the process of negotiation rather than to its effects. Nonetheless, some researchers have considered the role of the department chairman under collective bargaining, collective bargaining's effects on faculty morale, and its eventual effects on students. Many of these reports have been summarized in *Adjusting to Collective Bargaining* (Ernst, 1975).

Whatever its effects, collective bargaining is assured a place in community colleges. States are enacting legislation permitting bargaining by public employees; and faculty sentiment is, for now at least, definitely on its side. In the 1975 Faculty Survey, 43 percent of the respondents "strongly agreed" and another 25 percent "somewhat agreed" with the statement, "Collective bargaining by faculty members has a definite place in a community college." Fewer than 15 percent disagreed, with the remainder expressing no opinion. The data are consistent with those revealed in the 1972 ACE survey, in which 46 percent of the two-year college respondents "strongly disagreed" and 29 percent "reservedly disagreed" with the statement that collective bargaining has *no* place in a college or university (Bayer, 1973).

These data conform with the findings of such statewide studies as that conducted in Minnesota in 1968, wherein 62 percent of the two-year college faculty were favorable toward collective bargaining (Eckert and Williams, 1972). Whether or not collective bargaining modifies the faculty work environment, it is certain to expand at least for the rest of the decade (Bayer, 1973).

A profession is defined by those who work in it no less than by the way it is perceived by laymen. And the teaching profession cannot be separated from the institution in which its members work. The information in the following chapters offers a view of the way instructors see their own modes of professional functioning. The general impression is that they are not excessively concerned with their professional image. They are teachers first, members of the teaching profession second. Most of them leave questions of professional status to their nominal leaders. Still, as the instructors are compared with one another and as the entire group's pattern of relationships with their colleagues, students, administrators, and the ideas basic to their colleges emerged, the outlines of the group may be traced.

CHAPTER

2

SURVEYING
THE FACULTY

Gathering reliable data on two-year college faculty is a useful but precarious exercise. Many studies of people in higher education are limited by the heterogeneity of institutions, the difficulty of obtaining accurate samples, and the poor response rates to large scale surveys. Institutional diversity is a problem in itself. Since two-year colleges include private, liberal arts-related institutions of fewer than 200 students; new, public, occupational, and technical institutes; multicampus, comprehensive, colleges with over 30,000 students; colleges in rural areas drawing students from 100 miles around; inner-city colleges without campuses; and numerous other types, accurate data about faculty can be obtained only if a broad sample of colleges is utilized.

Even when a representative sample of colleges is drawn, what characteristics accurately portray the faculty within them? Distributing survey forms "to the faculty" in wholesale lots is risky; they may never reach their source. And asking someone on the campus to "sample" a number of instructors is irresponsible, especially if a particular subgroup is needed; the contact may pick the first ten coming through the door. To reach their target populations, questionnaires undoubtedly must be addressed to specific instructors; but because colleges do not uniformly maintain faculty data, accurate lists are not readily available. And although catalogues typically provide names of full-time teaching faculty, they are generally published well in advance of the school year and are, thus, out of date when in use. More important, part-time and adjunct faculty are usually not listed at all because, frequently employed at the last minute, their names may not be available until the term is well under way.

A third problem—the difficulty of obtaining responses to surveys of large populations—has been well-documented. A common practice is to mail out a huge number of questionnaires and accept a small proportion of returns. The undesirability of this procedure is evidenced by the numerous surveys reporting response rates of 20 to 30 percent. One can only speculate on the systematic bias among respondents in these samples. Some investigators control for low rates of response by "forcing" answers from a small number of nonrespondents and comparing them with the volitional responses. Others attempt to solve the problem by weighting the respondents within categories, thus leveling the returns.

Whatever the techniques to encourage responses, most data-gathering procedures are concerned with mailing questionnaires addressed to the sample population. Panos and Astin (1968) reported that autotyped special delivery letters produced higher responses at a lower cost per respondent (former students) than did registered mail, telephone calls, or mimeographed letters. And Rossmann and Astin (1974), comparing 14 mailing techniques, each subtly different, found that current and former college students were most efficiently surveyed using nonprofit outgoing postage, window envelopes, and business reply returns. The effect of offering cash rewards was noted by Dohrenwend (1970-71) and Hackler and Bourgette (1973); of precontact with respondents by Walmsley (1973) and Parsons and Medford (1972); of length of questionnaire by Champion and Sear (1969). The various procedures for increasing returns were summarized by Linsky (1975), whose survey of the literature found postcard reminders, precontact with respondents by telephone, type of postage, cash rewards, and the type of organization sponsoring the study all reportedly effective.

Those who survey college faculty similarly attend to problems inherent in obtaining reliable data. Some weight for nonrespondents; the American Council on Education's national faculty survey (Bayer, 1973) assigned categorical weightings to account for variations in response among such subgroups as doctoral degree holders and professors in large, research-oriented institutions. Others use intensive follow-up procedures; by so doing Leslie (1973) received just under 70 percent returns from a sample of Pennsylvania faculty (1974) and an 86 percent return from a sample of 100 Pennsylvania community college instructors. Higher return rates seem always to be obtained if on-site facilitators can deliver and retrieve the questionnaires—a technique employed frequently by such survey research organizations as the National Opinion Research Center and Field Research Corporation. Indeed, in a survey of two-year college faculty members, Bushnell (1973) obtained a 90.9 percent response by having a person on each campus collect the forms. But his methodology can be questioned in that the rate of return was severely inflated through the exclusion of 24 of the 92 participating colleges because they returned fewer than 75 percent, and because the on-campus facilitators were allowed to select their sample within prescribed limits.

METHODOLOGY

To mitigate these problems, the Center for the Study of Community Colleges was charged with doing a nationwide survey of humanities instructors in two-year colleges for the National Endowment for the Humanities. The objectives of our investigation required a sample that would be representative of both full- and part-time faculty members in the humanities, together with a comparison group of nonhumanities faculty—predominately, chairpersons. A further requirement was that the group be large enough to permit cross-classification of information by several variables simultaneously. A mailed questionnaire was the only method feasible within the budget, but it was deemed essential that representativeness be assured by following sound sampling principles, and that reliability be maximized by obtaining a high rate of completed questionnaires.

A two-stage sample—a broad sample of colleges selected at random within certain strata, and a sample of the faculty within those colleges—seemed potentially most useful. The main stratification variables for the colleges would be type of control (public or private) and geographical locale because these appear to be the main institutional differences affecting the faculty. Secondary variables included college emphasis (comprehensive, technological, liberal arts), organization (multi- or single-campus district), size, and age.

To ensure consistent definition of the population, a special list of faculty members teaching humanities in these colleges was drawn. Since the National Endowment for the Humanities excludes the performing arts from its purview, names were needed of people teaching courses in music literature/appreciation/history, but not those who, for example, taught performing music exclusively. Similarly, teachers in art history and appreciation were needed in the sample population, but not those in drawing, sculpture, or design. Theater history and appreciation were in; stagecraft and drama were out. Literature was in; reading and composition were out. Also needed were on-campus facilitators to forward necessary materials to the research team and to distribute and retrieve the questionnaires so the typical low response rate obtained in individual mailed surveys would not operate.

Several pilot tests were conducted to determine the feasibility of the methodology, the types of letters that should be addressed, the pattern of interaction with facilitators, and the responses that could be anticipated realistically. In one of these pilot tests, questionnaires were sent to 29 faculty members selected at random from rosters in eight college catalogues. This procedure, including one follow-up letter, yielded a predictably low return rate of 31 percent.

Five additional pilot procedures were tried, each addressed to eight different colleges. Three of the pilots used different types of letters addressed to the president of the college, one was addressed to the dean of instruction, and in one a personal contact was made through phone or letter naming a mutual acquaintance. In this latter procedure, we identified a person whom we knew and who also knew the president, and who could be named as endorsing the project.

The highest commitment to participate in the survey was obtained from the deans of instruction, but when this agreement was followed with the distribution of the questionnaires through these same deans, an extremely low rate of return was revealed. The lowest return rate in this piloting procedure was the one in which the personal contact was solicited through recommendations!

The pilot tests revealed that the president is the best initial contact point. In the pilot tests that went directly through the presidents, only approximately half of them agreed to have their colleges participate; when they did, however, from 88 to 94 percent of the faculty returned the questionnaires. The pilots were useful in that they revealed the potential for a high individual response rate by going through the president and employing an on-campus facilitator, and that one-half or more of the colleges invited would participate.

The next step was to determine the size of the sample. Previous research had indicated that approximately 20 percent of the full-time instructors in two-year colleges teach in the humanities. Although information on the part-timers was not available, a considerably lower number was suspected. Anticipating an 80 to 85 percent response, therefore, it was necessary to send out between 1,765 and 1,875 surveys to finally obtain the 1500 returns requested by the endowment. Within feasible limits, a large enough sample of colleges—about 150—was also desired to maximize the spread by type of college.

To obtain a stratified random sample of colleges, the first stage consisted of drawing names from the *1975 Community, Junior, and Technical College Directory* (AACJC, 1975b). Anticipating that about 60 percent of the presidents would acquiesce to the request to survey their faculty, it was decided to invite 240 colleges initially. The 1,184 colleges in the *Directory* are arranged alphabetically by the 50 states. Randomization by type of control and geographic locale was ensured by starting at a random point and taking every fifth private and every fifth public college.

The second stage was develop the sample of humanities instructors. The colleges listed in the *Directory* indicate a total of 162,000 faculty. Assuming the sample of 150 colleges—about 12½ percent of the total—to be proportionate by size, it was anticipated that they would have 20,250 faculty (12½ percent of the total). If 20 percent of the faculty were in the humanities, the colleges would yield a pool of 4,050 names. Because fewer of the part-timers were expected to teach humanities, however, it was anticipated that the colleges in the sample would number between 3,500 and 3,750 humanities faculty members. Accordingly, a large enough pool could be generated by sampling one-half of the humanities instructors in each college.

Letters were sent to the presidents inviting participation and requesting the names of contact persons to act as campus facilitators. Other letters were sent to the facilitators, asking each of them to send to the research center a college catalogue, a spring 1975 schedule of classes, and a faculty roster if one more up-to-date than the catalogue listing were available. The catalogue was needed because the course descriptions would isolate courses that properly fall within the purview of humanities courses as defined by the endowment. This proved useful in such areas as anthropology, where courses emphasizing cultures of man were desired, but not those focusing on physical anthropology. Similarly, a course entitled "Principles of Geography" would be included if it were described as a cultural geography course but not if it emphasized scientific aspects. The course schedule was needed so names could be drawn only of the people who were listed as teaching those courses in spring 1975. And the faculty roster was needed to check for first names and cross-check such information as departmental affiliation and chairperson status.

A roster of humanities faculty for each college was generated by separately listing all full-time and part-time instructors and picking a random one-half of each. In addition, one-third as many department and division chairmen outside the humanities were selected. For example, if a college had a total of 20 full-time and four part-time humanities instructors, the sample would include ten of the full-timers, two of the part-timers, and four nonhumanities chairmen, yielding a total of 16 subjects for that college. This procedure demanded a careful review of every class schedule, but it was felt to be essential to produce accurate rosters of people teaching one or more humanities courses in spring 1975.

After pulling the faculty sample for each college, packets were prepared for distribution by the facilitator. Each packet included a questionnaire, an envelope stamped "Confidential," and a larger envelope addressed to the facilitator with the faculty member's name on the outside. The facilitator gave a packet to each named instructor. The respondent was instructed to seal his completed questionnaire inside the confidential envelope, place it in the envelope addressed to the facilitator, and return it. The facilitator was instructed to check the respondent's name against the roster provided by the research team, remove the outer envelope, and return only the sealed inner-confidential envelope. In this way he could determine who had not responded. Yet, the instructor's anonymity of response was protected because the facilitator could not see the completed questionnaires themselves. After the facilitator had retrieved the envelopes, he returned them to the center. If any were still outstanding, he was asked to try to retrieve them. Contact with the facilitators was by both phone and letter. In no instance were the respondents themselves contacted.

One hundred fifty-six colleges, nearly exactly representative in terms of type of control, locale, size, age, emphasis, and organization, participated in the study. The anticipated 20 percent of full-time faculty members teaching humanities proved to be accurate. Of the part-time faculty in the colleges in the study,

10.7 percent taught in the humanities. The overall pool consisted of 2,384 mailed questionnaires; 2,008 were returned (ten were unusable), including those from the nonhumanities sample. Questionnaires were retrieved from 100 percent of the faculty sampled in nearly two-thirds of the colleges. Overall, the response rate was 84 percent. Based on the checklists that were returned from the facilitators, it was surmised that between 4 and 5 percent of the surveys were undeliverable because of inaccuracies in the schedules, last minute faculty substitutions, and such. Thus, a large pool of data was obtained with a minimal number of nonrespondents.

Although the procedure demands extreme care and rigor in selecting the samples and pursuing the returns, we feel it is essential if generalizations to the universe of faculty members are to be made. A response rate that finds only around 10 percent of those receiving the questionnaires failing to return them can be assumed to be an accurate representation of the population without weighting for respondent categories. And the stratification of colleges allows for cross-tabulations among respondents in various types of institutions, while still maintaining an accurate representation of the universe of institutions.

THE SURVEY FORM

The Faculty Survey, developed for the National Endowment for the Humanities' two-year college project, was designed to elicit a variety of responses that would eventually provide profiles of faculty teaching in two-year colleges. Based on a number of previously developed instruments, it was pretested on several subjects and underwent a number of revisions before being printed. This section discusses item design, preliminary testing, and final revision of the survey form.

One problem in test development is the difficulty in attributing credit. This is not because test developers choose to ignore other psychometrists and tests and measurement specialists but because so many questions have been asked in varied forms for so long that no one knows just when they first came into being. Thus, certain items appearing in the survey are revisions of ones taken from other questionnaires, developed either by other investigators or by us. Some items came directly from the American Council on Education faculty surveys, and one set—the Rokeach Terminal Values scale (1968)—was used with the permission of Milton Rokeach.

Several sets of questions were developed and tested with various groups: students in the University of California at Los Angeles Graduate School of Education and approximately 70 instructors in six community colleges in California and Florida. Many of the subjects responded to the preliminary forms by offering comments, and further revisions of the survey were made on the basis of affective reactions as well as cognitive impressions.

Additionally, third and fourth versions of the survey were submitted for criticism to several nationally known figures in the humanities as well as to the National Endowment for the Humanities' project director. In every case, attention was paid to the comments; and revisions were made on the basis of these comments. The final form of the Faculty Survey, which was administered according to the procedures discussed earlier in this chapter, is found in the Appendix.

Items in the faculty survey were arrayed in eleven major subgroups and were then divided into two sets: categories and constructs. The categories were demographic, experience in profession, and values. The eight constructs included: "preference for further preparation," "curriculum and instruction," "research orientation," "concern for students," "university as reference group." "concern with humanities," "satisfaction," and "functional potential."

Categories

Demographic

This category is comprised of the most common questionnaire items—information about age, schooling, academic field, family background. While rather a broad group, it is useful for obtaining general information and for developing subsets of individuals—for example, those teaching particular subjects, those who are above or below a certain age, highest degree earned, or such. Examples of questions fitting into this category include, "Were you ever a student in a community/junior college?" and, "About how many books were there in the home in which you were raised?"

Experience in Profession

Acknowledging an obvious overlap with demographic and professional involvement areas, this category attempts to ferret out attitudes regarding professional experiences. Along this line, one particularly important item asks for experiences and/or feelings of department chairpersons toward faculty holding the doctorate. Other questions include, "How many years have you worked in your current institution?" and, "Are you currently employed in a job in addition to your position at the college?"

Values and Attitudes

Throughout the Faculty Survey opportunities exist to express values and attitudes—albeit indirectly. This category attempts to elicit more direct reactions toward such situations as collective bargaining and affirmative action. Included are Rokeach's Terminal Values—a list of 18 values that the respondent rates according to importance. Other items ask for the degree of agreement with such statements as, "Students should not have representation on the governing boards of colleges and universities," and "Career education and occupational training should be the major emphasis in today's community colleges."

Constructs

Preference for Further Preparation

This construct is closely related to the previous category in that it is partially dependent upon actual experiences in both pretraining and in-service situations. Questions of attitudes regarding preparation and future plans are also included. Fitting into this subset are such questions as, "Would you like to take steps toward professional development in the next five years?" and, "What type of training would you seek before teaching if you were to begin all over again?"

Curriculum and Instruction

This strongly weighted construct is concerned with activities and attitudes regarding both curriculum and instruction. Here are found items directly relating to time spent in certain classroom activities and special awards received for outstanding teaching—for example, "Do you use a syllabus for teaching your courses?" and, "Do you usually distribute sets of written measurable objectives to your students?"

Research Orientation

Items fitting into this group assess the degree to which respondents are involved in or tend to prefer research and writing. Examples of items include, "Have you authored or coauthored a published book?" and, "Have you ever applied to an outside agency for a research grant to study a problem in your field?"

Concern for Students

Attitudes toward students are often quite removed from attitudes regarding preparation or even actual classroom experiences. In light of recent enquiries regarding research/teaching involvements in universities and colleges throughout the country, this construct may be especially useful for administrators and others who are in positions to hire faculty members. Included are such items as, "How would you rate the qualities that students should gain from a two-year college education?" and, "On your most recent working day, how many hours did you spend in student interaction outside class?"

University as Reference Group

To a greater or lesser extent, the way one conducts his/her personal and professional life is consciously or unconsciously dependent on the role models one holds. Personal orientation might vary considerably if the most viable reference group were colleagues rather than university professors. Here are found items as, "How would you rate the following as sources of advice on teaching?" (department chairmen, university professors, and such) and, "What has been your affiliation with professional organizations in the past three years?"

Concern with Humanities

This construct is geared to specific attitudes and feelings regarding the humanities, with a few items also included to assess direct experiences with these areas. Included are such questions as, "How do you experience the humanities other than through your teaching?" and, "How many courses do you think students in two-year occupational programs should be required to take?"

Satisfaction

This is a highly emphasized group, not only because we believe it represents basic personality characteristics but also because it portends ways in which colleges might become happier places in which to function. Although recognition is given to difficulties in attempting to isolate the basic orientations of satisfaction or dissatisfaction with life, an attempt was made to gain insight into such direct issues as relations with significant others, student behavior, and job security. Questions here ask for the extent of agreement with such statements as, "Satisfactory opportunities for in-service training are not available at this college" and, "If I had a chance to retrace my steps, I would not choose an academic life."

Functional Potential

This is a hypothetical construct that is built on psychodynamic principles of human functioning (Brawer, 1973b). Built on the constructs of development, maturity, and ego strength, this group is comprised of six fundamental traits: relatedness/aloofness, identity/amorphism, flexibility/rigidity, independence/ dependence, progression/regression, and delay of satisfaction/impulse expression. The amount of "functional potential" that the respondents possess is assessed by specifically including such statements as, "Teaching effectiveness should be the primary basis for faculty promotion," and "I belive that if I work hard, things will work out for me."

In sum, a questionnaire for the Faculty Survey was carefully developed, and a method that would assure a high rate of return was devised. The selection of the sample was undertaken so the survey findings would represent accurately the attitudes, background, characteristics, and work situation of the total faculty. Although the main sample was comprised predominately of instructors in the humanities—literature, history, political science, music, and the arts—a comparison group of instructors from other fields—predominately division and department chairpersons—responded to the same questionnaire. This non-humanities group included faculty in life and physical sciences, nursing, business, physical education, and all occupational and technological fields. A sample of part-time instructors was also drawn. When the data were tabulated, the differences among people in the various teaching fields proved less discriminating than did nearly all other measures; that is, the faculty are teachers first and humanists, scientists, or technologists, second. Accordingly, the data represent the faculty teaching degree-credit courses in two-year colleges nationwide. The following chapters recount the survey data and interpret them in light of other information about two-year college instructors.

3

BELIEF SYSTEMS:
ATTITUDES, VALUES

Since it is easier to obtain data about people than to gain insight into their feelings and attitudes and the conscious and unconscious biases maintained by everyone, most descriptions of college faculties offer demographic and/or experiential information. Thus we know much about instructors' ages, income levels, preparation sequences, degrees held, and credentials earned; considerably less about their feelings of satisfaction, areas of personal strengths and weaknesses, ultimate values, and attitudes toward life's purposes and directions. Nevertheless, such subjective information is vital to any understanding of the person; a mere count of the years he has spent in a particular activity is, as data on his height and weight, narrowly limited. Information on the types of schools an instructor has attended or the principal professional activities in which he has engaged becomes more meaningful when it is viewed alongside a report of his perceptions and attitudes. The person is a totality and must be viewed in terms of several dimensions, rather than an isolated few.

In our study of faculty in the two-year college, we attempted to answer questions about certain personality dimensions. How do our instructors view their relationships with significant others in their lives? With what other variables do these perceptions concur? Do the levels of satisfaction vary with age? Teaching experiences? With full-time/part-time status? In this and the following two chapters we answer these kinds of questions. Three personality-related or affective constructs are discussed in the Chapters on Attitudes and Values, Satisfaction, and Functional Potential. The rationale for employing these constructs, related literature, and Faculty Survey data are presented.

Although the terms attitudes and values are frequently used interchangeably, they can be separately defined. Attitudes are feelings about questions or issues; values are basic belief systems. Although both may be unconsciously held and not often overtly expressed, they are nonetheless central to human and institutional functioning because they may give rise to markedly different forms of behavior. Thus they are tied to education at all levels from the generation of policy to the interaction between teacher and student.

Many surveys collect information on attitudes; hence some information is available about the way two-year college instructors feel about their role and the institutions in which they work. One question often asked is how the faculty see their college's prime mission, that of providing equal opportunity for higher education to all.

The 1969 Carnegie study found 86 percent of the community college faculty agreeing with the statement, "Opportunities for higher education should be available for all who want it." This was a much higher percentage than that indicated by the faculty in other types of postsecondary institutions. A 1971 National Education Association survey, "Here's What Junior College Faculties Think," found about two-thirds of the faculty supportive of the idea that free public education should be extended through the two-year college to all qualified persons. And the 1971 Project Focus study respondents placed the goal, "Serve higher education needs of youth from local community" second on their list of 12 preferred goals (Bushnell, 1973). Apparently the faculty tend to agree with the policy of open access.

However, on closer examination, attitudes toward general questions sometimes change shape. As an example, the Carnegie Study found the two-year college respondents lowest of all the various faculty groups surveyed in their belief that education would be improved if "there were less emphasis on specialized training and more on broad liberal education." Further, in the Project Focus study, the faculty expressed their feeling that the prime goal of their college should be "Help students respect own ability and limitations," and they ranked the goal statement, "Provide some form of education for any student regardless of academic ability," seventh. Equal opportunity seems favored, but within certain restrictions.

Most surveys find two-year college instructors more conservative than their counterparts in senior institutions on political and social issues and more liberal in educational matters. The Carnegie study revealed a much higher percentage of two-year college instructors who felt that "Political activities by students have no place on campus," and that "In the United States today there can be no justification for using violence to achieve political goals." The two-year college population was lowest among all faculty groups in its characterization of itself as "left" or "liberal" on political and social issues, highest in the number of those who characterized themselves as "moderately conservative." This conservatism carries over into campus political issues; they were lowest of all groups in their agreeing with the statement, "Faculty members should be free to present in class any idea they consider relevant."

But despite their political conservatism, two-year college instructors are more likely to be in favor of collective bargaining and unionization. Collective bargaining has made greater strides among community college faculties than among faculty in any other type of postsecondary institution. Political conservatism and union activism apparently can go hand in hand. There are differences too among faculty in different teaching fields; the 1971 NEA survey found opposition to the use of the strike by faculty members lowest among humanities faculty, highest among faculty in technical areas.

Faculty attitudes toward teaching are noteworthy. Many of these were revealed in their responses to the Faculty Survey. A number of respondents indicated they prefer teaching small classes, and they said that teaching the humanities to students in occupational and remedial programs is different from teaching transfer students. They favored interdisciplinary courses but felt that knowledge in their field was expanding so fast that they needed further training to keep up. And although they felt that teaching the humanities to students in occupational and remedial programs is different from teaching transfer students, they believed that the same humanities courses should be given to humanities and nonhumanities students. In short, they have confidence that they can work out the differences within the confines of their classroom.

The faculty tend to favor other aspects of the general community college mission. More than 90 percent of them agreed with the statement, "This college should be actively engaged in community services." And 38 percent of the humanities instructors—a surprisingly high number—agreed that, "Career education and occupational training should be the major emphasis in today's community college"—this despite the fact that nearly 60 percent of them agreed that "The humanities are being diminished in importance in the community college."

Any split between faculty and administrators is not revealed in faculty attitudes in general toward institutional governance. The statement, "Overall, this institution's administration is creative and effective," was agreed to by 56 percent of the respondents. A sizable majority disagreed with the statement that "Students should not have representation on the governing boards of colleges and universities." And 61 percent disagreed with the statement, "The administration of my department is not very democratic." The move toward unionization often takes the form of a power struggle between faculty and governing boards but it is not reflected in individual instructors' attitudes toward the people with whom they work.

Faculty attitudes toward institutional mission are further revealed in their responses to choices regarding the qualities they think students should gain from a two-year college education. The ACE faculty surveys had found that significantly fewer community college instructors felt their teaching should lead students to develop creative capacities and the ability to pursue research. In the Faculty Survey, the statement that students should gain "An understanding and mastery of some academic discipline" drew the fewest responses as being a very important end for community colleges. Highest of all was the assertion that students should gain "Self-knowledge and a personal identity." This corresponds

with the ACE finding that more two-year college than four-year college instructors felt their institution should "Provide for students' emotional development."
In both the ACE and the Faculty Survey the belief that the community college
should lead its students to gain knowledge and skill directly applicable to their
careers achieved agreement by a sizable percent of the respondents. A similar
goal, "Help students adapt to new occupational requirements" was ranked third
in the Project Focus study.

There is a marked consistency among the faculty's perception of some
aspects of their professional situation. The 1972 ACE survey found 87 percent
agreeing with the statement, "Teaching effectiveness, not publications, should be
the primary basis for faculty promotion." In our Faculty Survey, 84 percent
agreed with that statement (although the phrase, "not publications," was left
out). The statement, "Faculty promotions should be based in part on formal
student evaluations of their teachers" drew agreement from 64 percent of the
respondents in the ACE survey, 62 percent in our Faculty Survey.

Whereas attitudes relate to the person's view of specific questions, the
values one holds are much more basic. They give rise to attitudes, but they
themselves are more underlying and enduring beliefs.

In recent years the study of values has been notably enhanced by the work
of Milton Rokeach (1968a). Rokeach defines a value as an enduring belief that a
specific mode of conduct or end state of existence is personally or socially
preferable to an opposite or converse state. For the purpose of measuring
values, Rokeach built two sets of scales focusing on the subjective ordering of
values rather than on the idea that value inheres objectively in some statement or
thing. His use of the terms, "Instrumental" and "Terminal Values," stems from
the definition that values are not simply discrete beliefs about desirable states of
being. Rather they are organized by each person into a system of priorities
according to those that the person cherishes as being of greater or lesser importance.

Of the two Values Scales developed by Rokeach, the Instrumental Values
suggest specific modes of conduct, while the Terminal Values suggest desired end
states of existence. Each of the Values Scales includes 18 statements, alphabetically arranged, along with a brief description elaborating the statement. Each
statement describes a good or desirable value. The respondent is instructed to
arrange the statements in order of importance to himself, or, as the directions
specify, how they appear "as guiding principles in *your life*." It is not easy to
rank the values, since the lists include nothing bad or undesirable. The list of
instrumental values includes such statements as, ambitious, broad-minded,
capable, cheerful, and clean. The list of terminal values includes, comfortable
life, equality, exciting life, family security, and freedom. All are desirable; each
respondent must rank them according to how he feels about them. The Values
Scales have somewhat the characteristics of a projective test because each
subject ranks the values according to his own internalized hierarchy.

The scales have been utilized with people in many different occupations. They have been given to policemen, Catholic priests and seminarians, service station dealers and oil company salesmen, recreational vehicle owners, and numerous other groups, in addition to their having been used with teachers and students at all levels of education. Not surprisingly, members of different occupational groups rank values differently. As an example, policemen place family security, a world at peace, and freedom at the top of their list; priests and seminarians see salvation, wisdom, and happiness as their most cherished values. Many of the differences among occupational groupings have been summarized by Fay (1976).

The Values Scales have been used several times among community college instructors. Faculty members in three California colleges responded to the scales in 1969 (Brawer, 1971; Park, 1971), and they were used in a study of staff members in Oregon community colleges in 1973 (Pritchett, 1973). In addition, scales were administered to elementary and secondary school teachers in 1972 (Sikula et al., 1972). The respondents to the Faculty Survey also ranked the Terminal Values Scale (Rokeach, 1968). Thus, there is quite a bit of comparative data.

The ranking of self-respect first by the respondents to the Faculty Survey corresponds with the ranking assigned to that value in the 1969 study of California Community College instructors. And salvation again comes up last, national security next to last, pleasure third from last, and social recognition fourth from last. In short, the topmost value and the bottom four are no different for the national sample in 1975 than they were for a group of instructors in three colleges in 1969. The changes that did appear are indicated in Table 1 showing the median rankings for both.

There are many ways of interpreting the value rankings in Table 1. One thing is notable: the rankings for faculty members at all levels of education are more alike than they are like the rank orderings ascribed by members of other occupational groupings. That is not surprising, but what is surprising is that faculty members tend to organize their value systems around self-oriented rather than socially oriented values. Freedom, defined as "independence, free choice," is consistently ranked considerably higher than equality, defined as "brotherhood, equal opportunity for all." Self-respect is tops; and the social value, a world at peace, is twelfth. The two-year college instructors certainly seem more concerned with their own sense of well-being than with social justice and peace for all mankind. The same holds true for elementary school teachers and for the university professors who responded to the scales.

The tension between the demands of society and one's sense of self has been seen as a concern that should be faced by people training professionals. Professional training has been cited as giving a person a world view that submerges his own values. Bloom et al. (1973) summarize the problem, stating that socializing forces of graduate training can be powerful and dehumanizing, that

TABLE 1

Terminal Values of Two-Year College Instructors

National Faculty Survey, 1975		Faculty in Three California Colleges, 1969	
N = 1493		N = 238	
Self-respect	1	Self-respect	1
Wisdom	2	Sense of accomplishment	2
Inner harmony	3	Freedom	3
Family security	4	Inner harmony	4
Freedom	5	Family security	5
Sense of accomplishment	6	Wisdom	6
Happiness	7	Happiness	7
Mature love	8	Mature love	8
True friendship	9	True friendship	9
Exciting life	10	Exciting life	10
Equality	11	Equality	11
World at peace	12	World at peace	12
World of beauty	13	Comfortable life	13
Comfortable life	14	World of beauty	14
Social recognition	15	Social recognition	15
Pleasure	16	Pleasure	16
National security	17	National Security	17
Salvation	18	Salvation	18

Source: Compiled by the authors, using Rokeach Terminal Values Scale. See Milton Rokeach, *Beliefs, Attitudes, and Values: A Theory of Organization and Change* (San Francisco: Jossey-Bass, 1968).

professional schools do more than endow people with competence to practice.

However, if the schools have such a marked influence, why are the basic values of the profession not paramount among faculty members? Is it that the graduate education experienced by instructors has failed to inculcate social values? The instructors see prestige and the fulfillment of personal needs as more highly desirable than the values their profession might reasonably be expected to promote. If the profession were dominant, one would think that a group of humanities instructors would rank a world of beauty higher than 13th! The Faculty Survey respondents might have been expected to place "aesthetic awareness" higher than fifth on their list of six qualities that they feel students should gain from a two-year college education. Bloom et al. (1973) say that the embryonic professional person has to fight hard to stay loyal to his own values in the face of professional education. The community college instructors seem to have won the battle.

The instructors' ranking of self-respect, wisdom, and inner harmony at the top suggest that they value the life of the mind or spirit ahead of social justice. Their placing "self-knowledge and a personal identity" at the top of their list of qualities that students should gain suggests that they are concerned that their students also value the personality as an autonomous center around which people should organize the various aspects of their lives. Wilson et al. (1975) similarly found humanities professors placing "self-knowledge and a personal identity" first among desired outcomes of a two-year college education. Certainly the difference in value structures held by faculty members and students are quite apparent—the same values lists given to students in the three California colleges showed marked disparity. Students were particularly concerned with such values as family security, a comfortable life, and an exciting life—values that suggest hedonism rather than harmony. If the faculty, then, value the more personal or spiritual, can they transmit these values to their students in the community college context? Do they try? And if not, where are the broader social values to be learned?

4

SATISFACTION AND
THE PERSON

For decades questions of job satisfaction have been pursued by industrial consultants. What leads to a person's satisfaction with his work environment? Are the basic elements in job satisfaction intrinsic or extrinsic? The reasons for the interest in these questions are obvious. As Frankel (1973, p. 1) notes, "Job satisfaction has been considered important not only for humanitarian reasons but also because it has been held that the person who likes his job will work with efficiency and enthusiasm—the dissatisfied one will show the opposite effect."

Although the theories of job satisfaction and the methods of studying this concept were developed in the business management field, the question has concerned researchers in education as well. In fact, in recent years, a sizable body of literature on teacher satisfaction has accrued. Some of it has been stimulated by faculty expressing concern about their working conditions as a backdrop to contract negotiations, and much has resulted from the curiosity of researchers who want to compare people in their own groups with those in other fields.

The community college faculty has received its share of attention. Compared with their counterparts in higher education generally, they seem better satisfied with their jobs. In the 1969 Carnegie faculty studies, 56 percent of the two-year college respondents felt "very satisfied" with the institution, compared with only 49 percent for the sample of professors at all levels (Trow, 1975). In studies of instructors in Minnesota (Eckert and Williams, 1972) and Florida (Kurth and Mills, 1968), 85 percent and 95 percent, respectively, expressed generalized satisfaction with their professions. Older instructors in Minnesota were found to be more satisfied than younger; vocational instructors were more satisfied than their academic colleagues; rural area people were more satisfied than those in the cities. In Florida, females who were older, married, and from rural backgrounds seemed more satisfied than their younger male counterparts.

Different conditions seem to influence satisfaction and dissatisfaction. Barrett (1969), observing that power and job satisfaction seem related, found that the degree of satisfaction among faculty in a North Carolina community college increased as their ability to make decisions concerning the college increased commensurately. Cohen asked community college instructors in California, Virginia, Maryland, Oregon and Washington to relate one incident that made them satisfied with their jobs and one that was displeasing or created dissatisfaction. He reports,

> Most of the instructors found satisfaction in feedback from their students. . . . [Indeed], more than 70 percent of the faculty in the Oregon-Washington group and in the two California colleges and more than 50 percent of the Virginia-Maryland group revealed gaining satisfaction from something to do with students. But only about 30 percent . . . suggested that dissatisfaction was related to their students. Instead, extrinsic variables, such as lack of support or interference from administrators or colleagues and institutional red tape, were noted as prime annoyances (Cohen & Associates, 1975b, p. 140).

Eckert and Williams (1972) also found the prime cause of dissatisfaction to be, "poor attitudes on the part of colleagues (p. 26)." In Wozniak's (1973) study of music faculty members in 64 two-year colleges, the determinants of job satisfaction were recognition, achievement, responsibility, the work itself, and relations with students. Such things as working conditions, supervision, and policy and administration generated dissatisfaction.

The literature on satisfaction among faculty in two-year colleges, while limited, does provide a way of looking at people functioning in a precise occupational setting. Indeed, job satisfaction may more accurately be reflecting the quality of life one experiences both within and outside the working environment. Further, satisfaction seems to be a pervasive characteristic more dependent on the individual than the situation, a dimension of personality rather than a reaction to a particular condition. Given the same situations, people vary in the degree of satisfaction they experience with them. In other words, satisfaction may be a basic *condition of* rather than a *response to* life.

Here, then, we postulate the notion that satisfaction is more closely related to the unique characteristics of the individual than to the situation or condition that elicits it. We suggest that satisfaction is a personality correlate rather than a situational response. We have, therefore, placed its discussion between values, attitudes, and "functional potential"—other discussions of personality.

What about the degrees of satisfaction possessed by the humanities faculty? To what other dimensions does satisfaction relate? A satisfaction index

TABLE 2

Satisfaction and Age

| | | | | Satisfaction | |
| | | | High | Medium | Low |
Age	N	Total (in percent)		(in percent)	
< 25	19	1.3	0.8	1.5	1.1
26–30	181	12.1	6.7	12.4	15.3
31–35	303	20.3	11.4	20.4	26.4
36–40	242	16.2	18.1	15.6	16.4
41–45	195	13.1	11.0	13.0	14.7
46–50	206	13.8	18.1	14.3	9.4
51–55	142	9.5	11.0	9.9	7.5
56–60	113	7.6	14.2	6.1	6.4
> 61	92	6.2	8.7	6.8	2.8

Note: Total N = 1493.
Source: Compiled by the authors, using 1975 faculty survey data.

was generated by aggregating responses to several items. The respondents were then divided into three groups—high, medium, and low satisfaction—on the basis of their relative score. Table 2 presents the relationships between people in each of the groups and other data.

Several of the observed relationships run counter to the findings of other studies, while others support them. For example, whether the respondent is a male or female seems to have little bearing on his/her degree of satisfaction. Nor are ethnicity and satisfaction related.

Age, however, is a different matter. The younger instructors—age 35 and less—are clearly more likely to be in the low satisfaction group; while the older teachers—from age 46 onward—are much more likely to be in the high satisfaction category. This is consistent with the findings in many studies and suggests either that by middle life those who were not satisfied with their lot had washed themselves out of the field, or that one becomes more resigned to life as one ages and this resignation may be expressed as satisfaction.

Years spent in college or university teaching do not seem to distinguish among people in high, medium, or low satisfaction groups, but years in teaching secondary school do. People in the high satisfaction group tend to be those who had taught five or more years in secondary schools. Similarly, the more years that one has been a faculty member in a two-year institution, the higher the level of satisfaction. Being a director of a special program has no bearing on satisfaction, nor does acting as a college administrator. However, currently acting as a chairperson is related; although only 15 percent of the subjects were heads of a college department or division, 19 percent of the high satisfaction group were chairpersons. Chairpersons tend to be older, but the status alone accounts for some of the variance. Members of this group apparently feel they have arrived. Highly satisfied chairpersons are more likely, too, to have employed people with doctorates and want to employ more of them.

A number of reports in the literature of the two-year college deal with the hours spent teaching. The inference is sometimes drawn that the more hours expended, the lower the rate of satisfaction. Our findings do not support this assertion, as Table 3 demonstrates.

By all accounts the part-time instructors should be less satisfied. Their wages are lower, they have little job security, and they tend to be given the left-over teaching assignments. But they are not. The proportion of full-timers and part-timers in the high, medium, and low satisfaction groups exactly parallels their proportion of the sample. But of the people who responded "yes" to the question "Are you currently employed in a job in addition to your position at this college?" more tended to be in the high satisfaction group than the medium or low. Higher proportions of those who were employed more than 21 hours outside the college were in the high satisfaction group. People with jobs elsewhere seem pleased with their role as part-time instructors. And the more hours

TABLE 3

Satisfaction and Class Hours Taught

Hours Teaching	N	Percent	Satisfaction		
			High	Medium (in percent)	Low
None	29	1.9	2.0	2.5	0.6
< 3	127	8.5	8.7	8.3	8.9
4–6	160	10.7	12.6	10.0	11.1
7–9	123	8.2	9.1	8.2	7.8
10–12	256	17.1	15.4	16.2	20.8
13–15	479	32.1	33.9	31.6	31.9
16–18	197	13.2	10.6	14.3	12.2
> 18	122	8.2	8.2	8.9	6.7

Note: Total N = 1493.
Source: Compiled by the authors.

they work outside the colleges the more likely they are to be satisfied. In brief, the person working full-time elsewhere is quite pleased to be teaching a class or two at the college level.

The reference group to which one adheres has something to say about both the group itself and the respondents. One way of ascertaining reference group identification is to ask who people look to for advice. People in the high satisfaction group are more likely to designate as "quite useful" all sources of advice on teaching. Those in the low satisfaction group consistently rank all eight reference groups as "not very useful." In other words, the people who are least satisfied with their teaching experiences are also disgruntled with all else in their environment. This suggests further the pervasive nature of satisfaction/dissatisfaction as an index of personality.

The relative level of a person's satisfaction is little related to his reading of scholarly or professional journals. However, more people in the high satisfaction group read four scholarly journals and one professional education journal. More in the low group read no journals in professional education.

When it comes to the type of training respondents would take were they to begin teaching all over again, 33 percent of the total reported that they would engage in the same programs they had attended. More people in the high satisfaction group (40 percent) so indicated, as contrasted with 26 percent in the low group. More people in the low group would have preferred taking more teaching methods courses and/or acquiring business or technical skills.

Since we suggest that satisfaction is basically a dimension of personality—even though one may reveal temporary reactions to a particular stimulus or environmental press—it seems likely that the less satisfied people would tend to want to change their occupations. This hypothesis is supported by the data. The satisfied faculty members are much less likely to say they would find "A faculty position at a four-year college or university," "A faculty position at another community or junior college," "A position in a professional association," or "A school outside the United States," very attractive five years from now. People in the low satisfaction group find all options more attractive. They are more desirous of moving away from both faculty and administrative positions in their own colleges. Similarly, the less satisfied instructors are less likely to be affiliated with professional organizations, although there is no difference in their tendency to go to meetings or present papers.

While an instructor's affiliation with a professional association may not be very important in terms of levels of satisfaction, his attitudes toward students are important. All the groups judged the qualities that students might gain from a two-year college education as important: "Self-knowledge and personal identity," "Knowledge of and interest in community and world problems," "Preparation for further formal education," "Aesthetic awareness," "Knowledge and skill directly applicable to their careers," and "An understanding and mastery of some academic discipline." However, a lower percent of the less satisfied instructors judged any of these as important. The groups were in accord on their assessment of the number of humanities courses that should be taken by occupational students. But, notably, the dissatisfied group consistently felt that too few noncourse-related presentations in the humanities were offered at their colleges.

Most respondents seemed to experience the humanities in similar non-teaching activities, and, with the exception of travel, the few differences are not noteworthy. Significantly, more people in the high satisfaction group than in either the medium or low groups noted "travel" as an approach to the humanities. Highly favored by large numbers were visits to art museums, shows, exhibits, concerts, theater, and film—half of all respondents.

The item regarding changes that had taken place already in the humanities failed to distinguish among the three groups. Most of the respondents (mostly the high groups) cited the addition or improvement of humanities courses. When it comes to the changes they would like to see effected, addition/improvement of humanities courses was by far the greatest choice for all satisfaction groups. Greater differences were noted with responses that opted for integrating humanities into interdisciplinary courses; the low and medium satisfaction groups tend to prefer them. This is particularly interesting in light of the many demands for interdisciplinary studies made in the literature and at conferences. More of the low satisfaction instructors also desire improved facilities and materials, more student interest in courses, more administrative support for the humanities, and (for a very small group of respondents) added ethnic studies. Greater numbers of the high satisfaction people indicate a desire to emphasize individual development and seminars, improved teaching techniques, and improved teaching conditions.

One of the items that has been used to distinguish groups of people in other studies (Brawer, 1973b; Cohen and Brawer, 1975a) is a group cohesion scale. This scale, which measures relatedness/alienation, has been incorporated into the construct of "functional potential." However, it also distinguishes among the three satisfaction groups on its own. Not unexpectedly, the degree of satisfaction correlates almost consistently with the respondent's degree of relatedness or alienation to a reference group. In all cases except for "My family," the high satisfaction group selects figures representing cohesion, while the low group selects anticohesion figures. In the case of the family as a reference group, a greater proportion of medium satisfaction respondents indicated relatedness.

Of the seven reference groups, "My group of friends," "My family," "Other instructors in my field," and "Most instructors in this school," warranted higher acceptance by most people (in order of responses) than did "My students," "Teacher organizations," or "College administrators" (again in order of relatedness). Family, friends, and colleagues are seen as closest to all satisfaction groups; the administrators, students and teacher organizations might be considered extraneous forces. By far, however, college administrators as a reference group discriminated the most among the three satisfaction groups, with "Most instructors at this school" running a not too close second.

These, then, are ways our three satisfaction groups line up in terms of specific items in the Faculty Survey. Other ways of interpreting the data may be useful for comparative purposes, however. For example, do types of schools differentiate among satisfaction groups? Does size?

While differences are not great, more people in the high satisfaction group are in public colleges; fewer are in private institutions. More of them are in comprehensive institutions as compared with vocational-technical or liberal arts colleges, more in schools that are older (founded in 1959 and earlier) than in more recently established institutions (either 1960–69 or 1970–75).

Size of school follows an erratic pattern. Whereas people in schools of 1 to 499 tend more to be in the high satisfaction group, the ranges from 500 to 999, 1,000 to 1,499, 1,500 to 2,499, and 2,500 to 4,999 indicate a reverse trend. With the larger institutions (5,000 to 15,000 and larger) more people are in the high than low satisfaction groups. Multicampus colleges claim a greater proportion of high satisfaction instructors than single campus schools or two-year divisions of four-year colleges.

Satisfaction is thus seen to be a dimension of the personality, not the environment. As a construct it correlates positively with "functional potential" (another personality measure), negatively with concern with the humanities, not at all with the constructs pertaining to the work situation. People who are less satisfied are alienated from students, colleagues, administrators, and all dimensions of their work. Those who are more satisfied are more related to their surroundings and to themselves.

Can satisfaction be enhanced? Brown and Shukraft (1971) offer an argument for environment modification, saying that self-reflection alone is "rarely sufficient to bring about change in the life of a person unless the social environment is supportive of such change. Just as there are mutually reinforcing aspects in the role of professor and student, there are reinforcing and constraining influences in the culture of a particular faculty" (p. 203). For Guion (1974), "Job satisfaction is a highly personal, subjective construct; different people react to the same organizational stimuli with different kinds and degrees of affect. Organizational climate, however, should be consistently perceived by different people; it is more objective. Climate is an organizational characteristic; satisfaction is an individual characteristic" (p. 294). In other words, we cannot deal with satisfaction directly, only with the environment that supports or denies the individual.

Nevertheless, in any viable institution it is impossible to ignore staff satisfaction, or the increasingly vociferous demands that institutions be more satisfying places in which to work. Jencks et al. (1972) argue that instead of evaluating schools on the basis of their long term effects, they be evaluated "in terms of their immediate effects on teachers and students. . . . Some schools are dull, depressing, even terrifying places, while others are lively, comfortable, and reassuring. If we think of school life as an end in itself rather than a means to some other end, such differences are enormously important" (p. 7). The issue becomes even more central when one considers the era of low growth so characteristic of academia in the 1970s. Relatively few full-time staff members are being employed, and few are leaving. It is nearly impossible to dismiss a disgruntled instructor, or to encourage him/her to resign or to be shunted to a quiet corner while handing over responsibilities to another staff member.

The way the Faculty Survey data were arrayed, people were placed into high, medium, and low satisfaction groups relative to each other. Therefore, we cannot say that faculty are or are not satisfied with their work. Nonetheless, both satisfied and dissatisfied faculty members are certainly found in the colleges. Typical staff selection procedures do not distinguish between them. Environmental modification that might ease dissatisfaction is rarely considered. The most hopeful note is that if satisfaction is a personality trait, each person may well have learned to live with his own tendencies. Relative satisfaction may not necessarily carry over into student learning or student affinity for, or disaffection with, the college.

The previous chapter offers the position that satisfaction is a dimension of personality only marginally related to the environment in which the person functions. Continuing our discussion of personality characteristics of instructors, this chapter discusses their "functional potential."

"Functional potential" is the core of a model of the person that was founded on theories of personality and on concepts of egopsychology. The model is divided into ten categories: "demographic variables," "environment," "group cohesion," "multiphasic characteristics," "orientations," "school directedness," "significant others," "values," "unconscious dynamics," and "functional potential." Since "functional potential" is the most important variable within the personality structure, it assumes the most emphasis in this structural model; it offers a nontraditional, unique way of perceiving people who have attained that stage of life we call adulthood.

Built as a construct especially for viewing higher education staff and students, "functional potential" has been used in assessing 1,800 freshmen in three California community colleges (Brawer, 1973b), in evaluating students in an experimental program operating within a community college (Cohen and Brawer, 1975a), and in our Faculty Survey.

"Functional potential" is based on psychodynamic principles of human functioning. It is expressed in the degree to which a person is able to tolerate ambiguity, delay gratification, exhibit adaptive flexibility, demonstrate goal directedness, relate to self and others, and have a clear sense of personal identity. It offers a picture of the functioning individual in terms of those personal dynamics that are basic to his or her behavior and lifestyle.

"Functional potential" is measured by aggregating certain items that represent six fundamental and bipolar characteristics, called modes. Although these modes are represented as dichotomous pairs, they do not imply either/or conditions, but rather ends on a continuum. We are here reminded of Jung's (1923) theory of the opposites, which suggests the presence of equally extreme but unconscious traits existing in the individual—each pulling in diametrically opposite directions.

The first of the six modes, relatedness/aloofness, indicates the degree to which an individual invests himself in involvement with others, his sense of belonging, or, at the other end of the continuum, his feelings of alienation. Identity/amorphism, the second mode, describes the sense of certainty about self that is possessed by the respondent. It is equated with feelings of wholeness, sameness, directedness, or, at the opposite pole, diffuseness and uncertainty of direction. Flexibility/rigidity measures the openness and closedness of belief systems as well as authoritarian attitudes. It includes both the cognitive and affective manner in which the individual approaches his life. Independence/ dependence suggests autonomy, the readiness to act on one's own; it does not imply separation or alienation from others, but it is closely tied to the first of three modal pairs. Progression/regression assesses one's orientation toward movement and change; it involves such traits as activity/passivity, fluidity/immobilization, and flow/fixedness and is related to the person's sense of optimism or pessimism. Delay of gratification/impulse expression, our sixth and final bimodal category, is best seen in mature individuals who have access to their more archaic impulses but are still able to exercise secondary controls when appropriate for the situation encountered.

The modes are not absolute ideals. The person who is operating best tends toward the first-named pole but demonstrates optimal functioning only when he is not completely isolated from the opposite extreme. Because the modes are more meaningful when grouped together to represent the entirety of the person, the scores are added to form a total, on which basis the subject is then assigned a high, medium, or low "functional potential" status. However, the extent or degree of functional potential demonstrated by any one individual is not absolute but, rather, both a stage and a goal. Even in an ideal world, every person would not be able to attain the highest level of "functional potential" possible, but at least he would be operating at his own highest level. He would also be aspiring to higher levels of actualization or individuation.

The ten categories then, with "functional potential" as the center, represent a way of looking at the person as a holistic, integrated pattern of complex dynamics and behaviors. By using this construct as a vehicle for assessing personnel--students, faculty, and staff—we deal with characteristics that are only minimally related to measures of intelligence or achievement. And in emphasizing dimensions of ego functioning, we maximize strengths rather than weaknesses, as is so often the approach taken in appraising others. "Functional potential" is a clinically sound, intuitive, global, and, in terms of administrative ease, feasible method for so looking at these populations.

Using this procedure, we assume that people reach different levels of development at different times. Within the populations that we have studied— particularly the freshmen—we have found some interesting variations in terms of developmental levels, attitudes and values, orientations toward life goals, and demographic characteristics. This diversity appears to extend beyond the rather narrow confines of the geographical area examined, Those freshmen, for example, who comprised the three college samples are considered to be representative of beginning students in community colleges as well as many four-year colleges and universities throughout the country.

Thus we have found that, while such quantifiable characteristics as the number of books in the home, hours employed outside school, and schools attended before the tenth grade differentiate types of students, "functional potential" cuts across many of the barriers commonly exaggerated and even encouraged by other assessment devices. At the same time, it does relate significantly to certain other variables. With the move from low to high "functional potential," for example, the students' school directedness scores increase, as did scores attributed to the impact of significant others and to group cohesion. Students who score high on "functional potential" appear more definite in their orientations and seem to relate more consistently to the established norm group on the Omnibus Personality Inventory (OPI) (Heist and Yonge, 1962). That is, the higher the "functional potential" scores earned by the students, the closer they are to the norm group on which the OPI was standardized, a group representing students in junior colleges, four-year liberal arts colleges, and universities.

When it comes to the dependent variable, dropout/persistence in school, "functional potential" acts an an especially useful predictor. In most cases, the first year dropouts among our 1,800 students tended to be in the low "functional potential" group. Students constituting the high group were less likely to withdraw from one of the three colleges than were those in either the low or medium group.

So much, then, for the theory and its validation. Within the two-year faculty, does "functional potential" differentiate among people in different age groups or different disciplines? How does it relate to demographic characteristics of people or institutions? What about this construct of personality and such variables as faculty satisfaction and attitudes toward the humanities? What about "functional potential" and other items comprising the Faculty Survey?

The "functional potential" index that was derived from our faculty questionnaire is comprised of 27 items, the respondent's index value being the sum of his scores on each of these items. High, medium, and low "functional potential" categories were established by deriving the mean score for the total group and placing the cutoff at one standard deviation above and below the mean. More people are in the high than the low group because, although "functional potential" was not developed on the basis of a normal distribution, it does act as a parametric measure, with the curve slightly skewed. This is not surprising because people who have shown sufficient ability to delay gratification have attained college degrees and are functioning as college instructors would be expected to be operating at higher than average levels of ego development. The normal curve distribution within the population sampled pertains, even though this population posed against the universe of adults would show a marked tendency to higher "functional potential" scores.

The faculty in different teaching fields display variant "functional potential" levels. More of the instructors who teach foreign languages and literature are in the low group than in the high or medium. Instructors of history, music, and religious studies tend toward the high group.

Although sex and ethnicity do not correlate with "functional potential," age does. The patterning is erratic, but functional potential tends to develop as the person gets older. This makes sense in terms of several theories of development and suggests that, as one ages, he develops the armamentarium to function in a more integrated fashion. The fact that people at age 61 or older tend toward lower "functional potential" suggests that in preparation for retirement, the older person may tend to "give up," to emphasize a stance of looking back rather than anticipating the future.

Some interesting conclusions can be drawn when "functional potential" level is plotted against experiences that instructors have had. Those respondents who had spent more than five years working in secondary schools tend to be in the high "functional potential" group. Those who had been in a university for less than five years tended toward the high group, whereas those who had had five or more years experience in senior institutions tended toward the low. The respondents who were currently acting as chairpersons tended more to be in the high "functional potential" group, a result pertaining both to the humanities and the nonhumanities sample. And, whereas 27 percent of the nonhumanities group were not chairpersons, people in that group made up only 14 percent of the high "functional potential" group, 47 percent of the low.

These data suggest a trend for people of high "functional potential" to move from secondary schools to two-year colleges, whereas people with low tendencies move from four-year colleges and universities to two-year institutions. Further, the people with low "functional potential" tend to stay in two-year colleges longer; and those with high tend to become chairpersons. The tendency holds both for the humanities and the nonhumanities faculty members. What the data are suggesting, then, is that the people who have come to two-year colleges from secondary schools are the well-integrated, involved individuals; those who have come from four-year colleges are not. They suggest also that if the people of high "functional potential" are to stay in the two-year college they need the kinds of challenges that go along with their taking leadership roles such as division and department chairmanships.

"Functional potential" differentiates also between full-time and part-time instructors. The full-timers tend more to be in the high group, while the part-timers are significantly more likely to be represented in the low group. Moreover, the high "functional potential" full-timers tend also to be employed at jobs in addition to their teaching. In short, well-integrated individuals are more likely to be involved in a greater variety of activities.

People with high "functional potential" tend also to see the people in their environment as important. The high "functional potential" instructors listed all choices of "Sources of advice on teaching" as "quite useful" more often than did the low people. Nevertheless, the high "functional potential" chairpersons were not those who also tended to want to employ people with doctorates. They used the argument that they would not hire such instructors because of the higher salaries they command.

The high rate of involvement in the profession exhibited by people in the high "functional potential" group carries through in their relationship to professional organizations. They tend to read more scholarly and professional journals, and they are more likely to be members of professional associations. There is a tendency for the high "functional potential" people to say they experience the humanities on their own through talking with peers or associates, attending classes or seminars, and everyday experiences, Apparently, their pattern of involvement includes a social dimension.

Differences also are found among the three "functional potential" groups in their plans for the future. In keeping with their need for challenges and additional responsibility, high "functional potential" instructors were considerably more likely to see the desirability of an administrative position in a community or junior college in their own future. The low "functional potential" group was much more likely to want a nonacademic position or a position in a school outside the United States. Nonetheless, "Doing what I'm doing now," was much more likely to be seen as very attractive by the high "functional potential" group than the low.

Past and future professional development also was perceived differently. The high "functional potential" people were more likely to wish they had been more involved in teacher training, studying humanities, doing more student teaching, taking more teaching methods courses or courses in psychology and personal development, and getting higher degrees. They tended more to desire further steps toward professional development in the future; 95 percent of the high group indicated this desire, whereas only 69 percent of the low group saw the usefulness of further professional development. Individuals in the high group were more likely to want to attain doctorates, and they tended to be over-represented in the group that was working on their doctoral degree at the time.

Just as high "functional potential" instructors saw the people in their environment as more useful, so they tended to see more value in all the choices of qualities to be gained by students at their institutions. All choices were more likely to be seen as "very important." Further, they tended to favor three or four humanities courses for students who are enrolled in two-year occupational programs. The low "functional potential" instructors were quite likely to hold no opinion regarding course offerings for these students. However, in the items pertaining to extracurricular activities, there was no difference between high and low "functional potential" instructors, except that members of the high group were more likely to see too few colloquiums and seminars. Further, they also indicated a preference for better humanities courses, more emphasis on individual development and seminars, improved teaching techniques, more student interest in courses, and greater student respect for the humanities. The high "functional potential" respondents seem to be aware of changes that had occurred in the curriculum at their own institutions. They were more likely to indicate that interdisciplinary courses had been established and that facilities and teaching techniques had been improved.

In the study of freshmen in three California colleges (Brawer, 1973b), institutions in three distinctly different types of environments were purposely selected. One of the colleges was an inner-city institution, one a suburban college, and one located in a remote rural area. Yet, "functional potential" for the students coming from these quite different neighborhoods and from different ethnic and socioeconomic backgrounds did not differ. What differences were found cut across the three types of institutions. Similar findings pertained in the Faculty Survey in factors relating to whether a college was public or private; or, despite its form of emphasis, its organization, or its size, whether "functional potential" was not a differentiating characteristic.

"Functional potential" is a way of assessing and describing the functioning individual. Those in the high group tend to be more involved in everything around them; in fact, "functional potential" correlates significantly with all the following constructs: "research orientation," "curriculum and instruction," "university as reference group," "preference for further preparation," "concern for students," and "concern with the humanities"—all the constructs used in the Faculty Survey except for "satisfaction."

The institution that has a sizable percentage of its staff in a high "functional potential" group is faced with its form of challenge. These people need the chance to assume responsibility, working on higher degrees, taking on special projects, exercising their need to be involved with all dimensions of the college and the community. They can accept the challenge because they are considerably more able to tolerate the ambiguity that goes along with a new effort. They want to work with their colleagues and with their students. They thrive on open-ended tasks. And unless they are presented with these new challenges, they may well tend to phase themselves out of their teaching positions.

6

CURRICULUM AND
INSTRUCTION

Curriculum and instruction properly occupy most of the attention the faculty give to college operations. Courses are usually initiated by instructors responding to changes in their subject area or to signals received from current and prospective students. The curriculum review process typically includes faculty members on the committees through which new and revised courses and programs must pass. Regardless of catalog descriptions, the faculty are the arbiters of the curriculum, translating course outlines into patterned activities. Finally, the instructional program, although nominally under the direction of an administrator, is really administered by the instructor of each course, who selects methods and objectives and, through his tests, specifies what the students shall learn.

Much has been written about the teaching orientation of the faculty at two-year colleges. These colleges are known as "teaching institutions," differentiating them from "research-oriented" universities. Indeed, the community college's commitment to the teaching/learning paradigm clearly overrides all supplementary goals and functions, both broad and narrow. No matter what else the instructor is expected to do, or whoever he must be, he must cause learning.

Comparisons of two-year college faculty with their counterparts at senior institutions invariably find the former to be more interested in teaching than in research and less interested in publishing or otherwise attending to the scholarly aspects of their academic discipline. Community college faculty are also usually characterized as being more willing to work on their teaching, changing courses in accord with varying student abilities and individualizing instruction where possible. The conclusion that university teaching is more subject-matter oriented and that the community college faculty tend to be student-centered has been articulated by numerous commentators.

Still, the community college faculty does not present a clear picture in comparison with teachers at other levels of education. University professors are frequently seen as being autonomous, entreprenurial individuals interested in scholarship in an academic area. Elementary school teachers project an image of concern for children, a desire to nurture, and an interest in adopting new materials and techniques in the classroom. Secondary school teachers are stereotyped as being parochial practitioners, resentful of administrator, parental, or collegial intrusion.

Regardless of the level of instruction, Wilson et al. (1975) point to the effective undergraduate teachers as not enacting their roles in a perfunctory manner, but rather in going well beyond their prescribed task of transmitting knowledge and skills to students.

> They are more committed to teaching, . . . and . . . they work harder at stimulating student interest in the content of the courses they teach. They more often exchange ideas with students regarding current social, political, and cultural issues and changes in the society at large. In this way they both respond to student desires for greater social relevance in their education and relate to students as partners in the learning enterprise. Moreover, the attempts of effective teachers to stimulate, to relate, and to educate are not limited to their classroom activities: they more frequently interact with students beyond the classroom as well, discussing careers and educational plans, course-related ideas, campus issues, and problems of immediate personal concern to individual students (p. 192).

The image of the community college instructor is not clear because the institution is still relatively new and images take a long time to crystallize. Further, the community college itself has shifted roles repeatedly and markedly during the tenure of many currently practicing instructors. It has gone from a subbaccalaureate institution to a vocational training center to a compensatory education institution to an adult education enterprise, returning to all the old purposes even while adopting the new ones. The faculty plaint is, "What is this place supposed to be doing, and what am I doing in it?" Consequently, the group as a whole maintains an indistinct self-image and projects an unclear collective picture to outsiders.

Nevertheless, teaching is the hallmark of the community college instructor. Many of them have become involved with instruction beyond the confines of their classrooms. Some have gone into public programming, building objectives and criterion tests around open-circuit television productions. Others have developed reproducible learning packages that can be used by students without instructor intervention. Still others have worked up computer-assisted instructional devices. If anything is happening in instruction in any school, some community college has a faculty member vigorously pursuing it.

However, the concept that instruction is a discipline of organized knowledge with its own theories, vocabulary, tested procedures, and operating methodologies has not taken hold in the two-year college. It is not prevalent in other types of schools either, except in certain specialized academies and training programs. The primary reason is probably that the practice of telling someone else how to do something is so common—most people do it frequently—that few teachers feel the need to go further into the rigors of instruction. Teaching is still conducted on the basis of, "If you know it, you can teach it."

There is a distinction between instructional theory and practice. Most instructors' involvement with instruction centers on the media of teaching and only peripherally—if at all—on assessment of instructional outcomes. Instruction is typically perceived as an activity, a transaction between a teacher or teacher-built program and a student or learner. Many instructors still see their own presence as the most important thing they can offer to the students; consequently they resist automated teaching devices. Others plunge heavily into the development of reproducible programs as a way of extending their own influence. In either case, though, the emphasis is on the media—whether reproducible or live—and not the intentions or results.

The utilization of specific measurable instructional objectives affords a case in point. The extent of the faculty's antipathy toward defined outcomes was revealed in a survey of department and division chairpersons in community colleges conducted by Hammons and Wallace (1976). The chairpersons were asked what they thought would be important for them and their counterparts to learn about managing curriculum and instruction. The respondents indicated that they were not overly capable in directing faculty, evaluating instruction, or organizing feasibility studies for new courses. Most felt deficient in the knowledge of nontraditional instructional approaches and in assessing the effectiveness of various instructional strategies. Half felt seriously deficient in the knowledge of preparation of self-instructional materials, the use of instructional objectives, and the selection and use of media. Nevertheless, half the group felt either a "low need" or "no need" for instruction in the use of instructional objectives or in the writing of test items. The implication was that matters directly related to instructional processes are better left to individual faculty members—in short, catch as catch can.

Other studies of instructors revealed similar patterns. Guth's (1970) observation that behavioral objectives are not widely accepted by two-year college instructors of English, since the goals of English are long range and cannot be described in terms of skills, provides us with insight into at least some instructors' predilections. Hinkston (1968) comments that most history teachers give quick-score tests exclusively not because they are best for students but because they are easier to grade. Larson (1970) sums the issue of objectives and testing by pointing out that the kinds of gains that the instructors in the humanities seek rarely may be observed visually, let alone quantitatively. Millett (1973) discussed instruction with a number of faculty members in political science only to find that they typically avoid collective decisions about what is to be taught and how and to what purpose. For all the writing about the community college as a teaching institution, the faculty as dedicated professionals, and instruction as a discipline, in practice, many commentators report that instruction is still an individualized transaction, not amenable to management, public display, or communication in terms that have a clear and common referent.

There is certainly no unanimity of opinion, however; and the contrary view is often seen. Some reports suggest that instructors are concerned with devising new courses and revising existing courses so students can take away something of value. In some institutions, foreign language courses are being revised away from a grammar and reading emphasis and toward an applied approach, even to the point of offering career-related courses. Literature courses are often revised to include contemporary works as a way of stimulating student interest. Many methods of attracting students to history courses are being tried, including relating major themes to the students' life experiences, providing topical seminars, and combining the explicit statement of behavioral objectives with a modular schedule. Specific objectives are also used in political science and in other areas where self-paced individual studies projects have become popular.

The move toward modular scheduling and individualized courses has also stimulated a move in the direction of the best principles of instruction. Where students are required to view video-taped lessons on their own time and pass corresponding examinations, the course planners usually take great care that the course objectives, media, and examinations all correspond closely. Field work, too, has come in for its share of concern. Highly successful anthropology courses have involved students in archeological explorations on-site or in off-campus interviews of members of special population groups. Also, interdisciplinary courses have become popular in history and in the humanities.

In the main, community college instructors tend to believe that they are deeply involved in their teaching. They see themselves as concerned for students and for curriculum and instruction. A sizable majority of the faculty responded positively to queries about their teaching. Following are several items and their corresponding responses:

	Yes	No	N/A
Do you use a syllabus for teaching your courses?	72.8	25.6	1.6
Have you revised your syllabus and/or teaching objectives in the past three years?	92.7	5.0	2.3
Do you sometimes run an item analysis on a test that you give to your students?	49.8	46.7	3.5

	Yes	No	N/A
Do you usually distribute sets of written measurable objectives to your students?	47.4	50.0	2.5
Have you ever prepared a replicable or multi-media instructional program for use in your classes?	41.5	56.4	2.1
Do you typically submit written evidence of student learning (other than grade marks) to your dean or department head?	16.9	81.4	1.7

Further, when asked how they would spend their time if they had free choice in the matter, twice as many instructors said they would rather be spending more time in classroom instruction than less. Nearly half the group would like to spend more time in planning instruction; and 13 percent would like to be spending more time reading student papers or tests, as compared to 18 percent who would prefer less time in this activity. Eighty-four percent of the faculty tend to agree with the statement that teaching effectiveness should be the primary basis for faculty promotion.

As a way of assessing the extent of faculty concern for the more involved aspects of teaching, a construct entitled "curriculum and instruction" was developed. Items in the construct have to do with the instructors' teaching practices and preferences. High weights were given to those who responded positively to such questions as "Have you ever received a formal award for outstanding teaching?" "Do you sometimes run an item analysis on a test that you give your students?" "Have you ever prepared a replicable or a multimedia instructional program for use in your classes?" Those respondents who also indicated that they would prefer giving more time than they currently do to classroom instruction or to planning instruction were also scored high on "curriculum and instruction." Other items included in the construct had to do with the type of training the instructor would seek if he were to begin teaching all over again; here those who would have taken more teaching methods courses or done more student teaching were considered to be interested in "curriculum and instruction." Several items of opinion were also included in this construct, such as, "I prefer to teach small classes." Here a negative response was considered a positive in terms of the construct.

Those faculty members who placed high on the "curriculum and instruction" construct tended to be the full-timers with three or more years experience in community colleges, especially those currently working on a doctorate degree. They tended to see all groups as useful sources of advice on teaching. They tended to read professional education journals, and they were members of and attended meetings of professional organizations. They said they would like more professional development and would find administrative or professional association work attractive. Members of this group tended to be those who were former students in community colleges.

The possession of a doctorate did not seem to differentiate among people highly concerned with "curriculum and instruction." Nor was there any difference among people working in public or private colleges, colleges with one or another emphasis, or those with more or fewer students. However, for the non-humanities group, the people with former experience in four-year colleges and universities tended to be higher on this construct. Perhaps they found the four-year college unattractive because of its emphasis on scholarship and research and went to the community college, where they knew that a focus on teaching was expected of them.

As might be expected, those respondents occupying positions as chairpersons of their division or department scored high on the curriculum and instruction construct. The longer they had been chairpersons, the more likely it was that they would be in the high group. Either the experience of being a chairperson lends one to focus more on curriculum and instruction, or those who tend to emphasize portions of their work that fit with the discipline of instruction tend to become chairpersons. The chairpersons high in curriculum and instruction also tend to be those who plan to employ people holding doctorates.

Significant relationships were found between the instructors high in concern for "curriculum and instruction" and several of the other items in the survey form. The group tended to feel that the most important qualities students could gain from a two-year college education were "self-knowledge and a personal identity" and "aesthetic awareness." However, the nonhumanities group put "knowledge and skill directly applicable to their careers" first, and "understanding and mastery of some academic discipline" and "preparation for further formal education" at the bottom of their list. Apparently the high "curriculum and instruction" group adhere to those community college goals that fit their own area of teaching responsibility. The humanities instructors high in this construct also believe that there there were too few colloquiums and seminars, exhibits and concerts, and recitals in the humanities at their institutions.

The high curriculum and instruction group tended to relate to other instructors at their own school and to teacher organizations, students, and administrators. Thus, it is not surprising that members of this group were also very high on "functional potential" and on "concern for students." The very high correlation among these three constructs suggests an involved practitioner, self-integrated, concerned with his teaching and his students. There was also a positive correlation between "curriculum and instruction" and "concern with the humanities"; those who are concerned with the curricular aspects of their work should also be concerned with a discipline in which they are teaching. But the high concern with the humanities held also for the nonhumanities faculty members who were high on curriculum and instruction, thus suggesting that people in any discipline who are intensely concerned with their teaching responsibilities also see a place for the humanities.

Other positive correlations were found between "curriculum and instruction" and "satisfaction." Undoubtedly, the most highly satisfied people in community colleges are found in the ranks of those who are concerned with teaching. There was also a positive correlation between "curriculum and instruction" and "research orientation." "Research orientation" in two-year colleges may well be interpreted as research on teaching, rather than research in an academic discipline; hence, this relationship might be expected. There was no correlation between the "curriculum and instruction" construct and the construct of the "university as a reference group."

One of the surprising findings in viewing the "curriculum and instruction" construct was that the foreign language teachers tend to be low, the history instructors high. Some of this may be accounted for by the fact that part-time faculty are more highly represented in foreign languages and quite low in history; that is, the difference in the construct may be due less to the academic discipline affiliation and more to the full-time/part-time status of the individual.

In sum, the two-year college faculty includes a number of persons deeply concerned with various aspects of their teaching. They adhere to the best principles of instruction, giving attention to objectives and results, as well as to media. Members of this group are satisfied teachers, concerned with their students and the role of their institution. They are the instructors who are building their profession and their profession's image.

CHAPTER

7

CONCERN FOR
STUDENTS

Spokesmen for community colleges proudly see their schools as teaching institutions—concerned with modes of teaching and with student progress. They care for students, not research; for information transmission, not knowledge generation. Thus they differ from the universities.

The literature about two-year colleges is consistent on the question of relative emphasis on teaching. Garrison (1967) saw junior college instructors as student-centered rather than subject-centered. More recently Wilson et al. (1975) made the same point, reporting that the subject matter approach or characteristic of the university is contrasted by the student-centered approach of the community college, where faculty are more willing to individualize their teaching. Instructors are seen as wanting to help students, although they may not always be able to do so.

This position has a long history, predating the student unrest movements of the middle and late 1960s. While the vociferous cries for relevance, for individualized treatment, for understanding on a deep and meaningful level had their effects on the universities, they only marginally influenced the community colleges. The courses on demand and the awareness of individual differences in two-year college classrooms had been already established. And the more recent emphasis on community education is only a thrust toward a broader embrace of students, wherever they may be.

Easier said than done, however. Gaff (1975, p. 4) says one of the problems is that "faculty typically long for bright and highly motivated students and hold that the quality of education would be improved if admissions requirements were higher or if grading were more rigorous." The problems of instructors who must cope with many students, some of whom are classified as remedial, are legion. Such students, a fact of community college life in the 1970s, will continue to populate the two-year college despite any hopes instructors may cherish for independent knowledge-seeking learners. At the same time, overt acknowledgment of a heterogeneous population, accepting all students as the human beings they are, and genuinely committing themselves to furthering their development, may provide tremendous rewards to instructors. By putting their own person on the line, they may not only help students, but also their own growth as professional beings will certainly be enhanced. This challenge can be most rewarding.

Many instructors have adopted the concept of functional equality, which implies a sense of relatedness, as a way of dealing with their students. This construct actually refers to basic attitudes, to the way people honestly see themselves, not merely to the physical arrangements of a classroom or lecture hall. It incorporates a humanistic relationship between teacher and student on a coequal basis. It acknowledges the fact that a person can be alone, indifferent, or closely connected in a crowd or in a tete-a-tete. There may be rapport between the instructor and the many hundreds of students to whom he is lecturing, while there may be aloofness and alienation in a one-to-one situation. It is not the structure that gives rise to interactions, but the feelings, the sense of openness, and the desires that exist within the people who are involved. The instructor who acts as mediator builds on these feelings.

He sees his primary function—and, indeed, often his exclusive function—as one in which there is direct intervention with students. Consciously or not, he focuses on the processes of human development; while conceptually, his very existence depends on the element of interaction itself. Although the teacher as model may be perceived separately—apart from the audience—the mediator must actually intervene with others, becoming an integral part of his students' lives while at the same time he feels they are equally a part of his.

The assertions about instructors' concerns are rarely tested, but here we differentiate among instructors who are more or less oriented toward their students. This chapter reports on instructors in the high, medium, or low "concern for students" construct; it relates this construct with others; and it examines relationships between degree of concern and selected items from the Faculty Survey.

The "concern for students" construct is comprised of several items coalescing around the instructor's orientation toward students. We believe that attitudes toward students may be quite removed from attitudes regarding previous preparation sequences or even actual classroom experiences. Since there have been frequent enquiries into the relationships between research/teaching involvement in some universities, we believe that this construct may be especially useful for administrators and others who are in positions to hire faculty. (Items comprising this construct and others, together with measures of central tendency and the assignment of scores to high, medium, and low groups, may be found in ERIC document ED 121-358.)

We might assume that concern for students has nothing to do with the teaching discipline—that is, that involvement with students and teaching field are unrelated. But we find that more people teaching art and liberal arts tend to be more represented in the high "concern for students" category, while foreign language, music, and philosophy instructors are more highly represented on the low end. And holding a graduate major in art or education suggests a greater tendency to be in the high group, whereas majors in history and music suggest the opposite. Faculty who had themselves been students in community/junior colleges tend to show more concern for students.

More females than males fall into the high "concern for students" group. Age, however, is an inconsistent determinant. Of the few ethnic minorities in our sample, more blacks/Negroes and Mexican-Americans/Chicanos are in the highly concerned group. Some relationships do exist between academic experiences and concern for students. For example, if one had been an instructor or administrator in a secondary school for one to four years, he is more likely to be in the highly concerned group than if he had been so employed five years or more. These same tendencies pertain to being an instructor or administrator in a four-year college or university, but not to the years spent as a faculty member in a two-year college. Here people who had been employed three to 10 years tended to be more concerned with students, while those employed 11 to 20 years were more likely to be in the low concern group. Faculty who worked in their current institution one to ten years tended to fall into the high concern group. Those so employed 11 to 20 years, however, were more likely to fall into the low group.

When it comes to department or division chairpersons an inverse relationship exists; people with either no or little such previous experience tend to be more concerned with students than those with experience. This tendency reverses itself when it comes to current status as chairpersons. Of the 15 percent who were currently acting as chairpersons at the time they responded to the faculty survey, 19 percent fell in the high group and 15 percent in the low group. A greater number in the high group had employed people with doctorates and planned to so do—even though some commented that doctorate holders are less interested in teaching than their nondoctoral colleagues.

People in the high "concern for students" category tend to read more in the professional literature and to belong to professional organizations. The construct is also related to professional development. We find that, whereas 86 percent of the total humanities population respond in the affirmative to the question, "Would you like to take steps toward professional development in the next five years?", 92 percent of the people in the high concern group and 73 percent in the low so respond. The types of steps desired also vary, and are inconsistent in their direction. More of the low group report they would like to enroll in courses in a university; more of the high group say they would like to obtain a higher degree. Responses to our question about training they would seek before teaching were they to begin all over again resulted in some interesting free responses. The instructors with low concern tended to say they would

TABLE 4

Primary and Secondary Goals of an Undergraduate Education
as Viewed by Faculty Members
(in percent)

	Community College	State College	State University
Knowledge and skills directly applicable to student careers	31	37	37
Understanding and mastery of some specialized body of knowledge	13	24	31
Preparation for further formal education	22	17	14
Self-knowledge and personal identity	53	33	30
Broad general education	56	59	61
Knowledge of and interest in community and world problems	20	22	21

Source: R.C. Wilson, et al., College Professors and Their Impact on Students (New York: Wiley, 1975), p. 20.

change nothing, but the high concerned ones inclined to say they would study humanities, do more student teaching, take more teaching methods courses, and take more psychology/personal development courses.

The group's perceptions of curriculum vary also. In the survey conducted by Wilson et al. (1975), the faculty responses to questions about the qualities students should gain were as shown in Table 4.

The goal of self-knowledge and personal identity was most highly favored by humanities professors, while the career preparation goal was most highly favored by faculty members in the natural sciences and the professional applied fields. And, whereas 46 percent of the humanities and social science instructors would give students voting rights on committees, only 30 percent in the professional fields would do so.

In our own Faculty Survey, we find somewhat different responses between the high and low "concern for students" group to five of the same and one different choice. Percentages for the selection "very important" to the six alternatives offered are as shown in Table 5.

The group low in "concern for students" tend more to see the academic discipline and preparation for further formal education as more important. The high group choose self-knowledge, aesthetic awareness, and knowledge of community and world problems.

TABLE 5

Important Qualities and Their Concern for Students

| | Concern for Students | | | |
| | Total | High | Medium | Low |
Qualities Ranked as "Very Important"	%	%	%	%
Knowledge and skills directly applicable to their careers	76.9	77.7	77.8	72.2
An understanding and mastery of some academic discipline	63.6	58.8	63.7	66.0
Preparation for further formal education	80.4	73.0	81.1	81.7
Self-knowledge and a personal identity	89.0	93.2	90.8	78.4
Aesthetic awareness	76.8	83.8	77.9	67.6
Knowledge of and interest in community and world problems	83.3	91.9	83.5	76.8

Source: Compiled by the authors.

The number of humanities courses that the faculty think students should be required to take does not differentiate between the high and low "concern for students" group. But in all cases, people in the low group show a much lesser tendency to respond "too few" to noncourse-related activities. They see a sufficient number of extracurricular programs; the high group sees too few colloquiums and seminars, lectures, concerts and recitals, and films. The high group tends to prefer interdisciplinary humanities courses and would like to see more individual development courses and seminars for their students.

We would expect that people high in "concern for students" would appear more related to their students on a measure of group cohesion than are faculty who are low in this variable. So they are. But our findings also show that people in the high concern group tend to be considerably higher in their relations to all reference choices. This leads to the conclusion that affinity for students may well stem from a general concern for others. It is a pervasive quality. Thus, "concern for students" reflects an extroverted, other-directed characteristic that transcends beyond students to embrace most of the significant others in the faculty members' world.

People high or low in "concern for students" may be found in any type of college; they do not cluster in the public or private institutions or those emphasizing comprehensive, vocational, or liberal arts education. A noticeable difference, however, does relate to the age of the institution. In schools built from

1970–75, 12 percent of the total population were in the high concern group and 4.0 percent in the low. In 1960–69 schools, 51 percent were in the high and 44 percent in the low groups; whereas in schools with a 1959 and earlier beginning date, 37 percent were in the high and 52 percent in the low group. People in the newer colleges may be more enthusiastic.

One would expect "concern for students" to relate positively with certain other constructs, and it does. It correlates almost perfectly with "functional potential" and with "curriculum and instruction." There is a high positive relationship between "concern for students" and "satisfaction," "concern with humanities," and "preference for further preparation"; a low positive relationship with "research orientation"; no significant relationship with the "university as a reference group."

The two-year college faculty includes a number of faculty who care about students. That assertion is not in contention. But it is interesting to note who these instructors are and what else they care about. The respondents in the high "concern for students" group tend to be those new to the college, themselves former two-year college students. They are involved professionally and would participate in in-service programs. They would like to see more interdisciplinary courses for their students and more extra-curricular activities so students would gain greater personal benefits. As for themselves, the faculty who tend to care more about their students are also highly satisfied, well-integrated individuals. They care about their teaching, not much for research.

CHAPTER

8

RESEARCH
ORIENTATION

Research is the activity that most markedly separates two-year colleges—whether public or private, comprehensive or technical—from the university. Community/junior colleges frequently boast research offices or directors of research who more or less rigorously conduct institutional studies on community needs, student characteristics, and enrollment/retention/attrition. Seldom, however, does an individual faculty member conduct research on his own—at least not unless he is engaged in a doctoral program and is collecting material for a dissertation. With this exception, the instructor at the two-year level of higher education hardly ever systematically examines a problem and/or publishes his findings. This stance has become so commonplace, in fact, that E. A. Dunham states "The research oriented Ph.D. is highly inappropriate for the community college teacher" (1970, p. 43).

The ACE 1972-73 survey of two- and four-year college instructors revealed that 87 percent of the two-year college respondents had published nothing in the previous two years, compared to 57 percent of the total group (Bayer, 1973). It also found that fewer community college instructors felt they needed better research facilities or more time for research. In addition, both two- and four-year college faculty members agreed that publishing should be considerably less important in the community college than in universities.

English instructors are the exception in that they do comment on their work and publish more than their proportionate share of articles. An extensive review of the literature (Cohen 1975a; 1975b; Cohen and Brawer, 1975b) found that a full quarter of the journal articles pertaining to the humanities in two-year colleges had been written by English instructors. Running a close second by proportion were the foreign language instructors. The other disciplines are far behind, with only an occasional article appearing in each subject field.

Several journals specialize in publishing articles written by two-year college instructors, for example, *College Composition and Communication* and *Community College Social Science Quarterly*. The articles in these journals frequently relate to problems of teaching, the area of concern deemed most appropriate for a two-year college instructor's research emphasis. Rarely does an instructor break into print in the strict disciplinary research journals.

Should a community college instructor do research? Certainly his instituion's commitment to teaching demands that he endeavor to predict, control, and assess the effects of his instruction. His research should be about his teaching. Does research interfere with teaching? In the late 1960s many vociferous university students complained that their professors were so busy doing research that their teaching duties were neglected. However, the charge has never been leveled at the two-year college instructor, and there is much doubt as to its credibility in the senior institutions. A Tufts University study found that publications and awards relate positively to ability in teaching undergraduate students and that funded research activities do not detract from classroom teaching effectiveness. Indeed, students at Tufts rated as their best instructors those who had published articles and had received government grants and/or other support (Bresler, 1968).

Although placing research and teaching at opposite ends on a scale has similarly been shown to be a false dichotomy elsewhere, people who are oriented toward research may differ from those who are not. If they do, how are they different? Are people interested in research as concerned with their students, for example, as those who are not? Does an orientation toward research correspond to a generally greater involvement with people and with other aspects of one's professional life?

Fourteen items in the Faculty Survey were scored together to form a construct called "research orientation." Examples of some items included are "Have you authored or coauthored a published book?" "Have you ever applied to an outside agency for a research grant to study a problem in your field?" "On your most recent working day how many hours did you spend in research or professional writing?" Responses were weighted, and instructors placed in high, medium, or low groups.

The people in the high research orientation group tend to be full-time faculty members, desirous of obtaining higher degrees. They are older and more likely male then female. And although they may be found in all sizes and types of colleges, there is a slightly greater proportion of them in the larger institutions. Since certain fields stress research more than others, we assumed that that variable would rather strongly differentiate among people in the various teaching disciplines. Our findings are not so dramatic, however, We find, for example, that 10 percent more history; 4 percent more anthropology; 3 percent more art and religious studies; 2 percent more liberal arts; and 1 percent more philosophy and social science instructors are in the high than low "research orientation" group. On the other hand, the low group claims 8 percent more foreign language, 5 percent more political science, and 3 percent more literature and music instructors.

Recording the number of books in the home in which one was raised has been used in some studies as a measure of socioeconomic status. While our own use of this item in the Faculty Survey did not yield consistent results, it would seem that the item should relate to "research orientation." That is, we expect that the number of books an instructor grew up with might directly influence his interests in research and writing. This assumption is supported. Whereas more people who had 11 to 200 books in the home in which they were raised were in the low "research orientation" group, more claiming over 200 books were in the high group (48 percent; 35 percent).

Years spent in a secondary school as an administrator or faculty member has little to do with "research orientation." Years spent in universities, however, is related. Of the respondents in the high group, only 39 percent had *not* spent any time at four-year colleges or universities, as compared with 64 percent of the low group. One to two years was spent by 18 percent of the highs and 9 percent of the lows; three to four years by 12 percent of the highs and 6 percent of the lows; five to ten years by 13 percent of the highs and 5 percent of the lows; 11 to 20 years, 7 percent high and 3 percent lows; and over 20 years, 3 percent high and less than 1 percent low.

Even more interesting is that while there are the same number or a greater percent of lows than highs who had spent up to ten years in the two-year college, 23 percent of the highs and 11 percent of the lows had been so involved 11 to 20 years; and 5 percent of the highs and 3 percent of the lows, over 20 years. Similarly, more people in the high than low group had spent 11 or more years in their current institutions. An orientation toward research is apparently not the new teachers's tendency, but grows with length of service.

Division and department chairpersons tend also to be oriented toward research. Only 15 percent of the respondents were chairpersons, but 25 percent of the high "research orientation" group were. However, there was no relationship between research orientation" group standing and those who tend to look to department chairpersons as useful sources of advice on teaching. The people in the high group were overwhelmingly biased in favor of professional journals and programs of professional organizations.

Not surprisingly, the high "research orientation" group shows an affinity for the university. They tend to see a faculty position in a university as attractive and would like more professional preparation. Those who were department chairpersons prefer employing people with doctorates, feeling they are more capable.

There is little relationship between "research orientation" and "satisfaction"; but people in the high group have an affinity for, and would like to become, college administrators or professional association representatives.

Apparently, although they like what they are doing, they see benefits accruing to their moving out of their current positions.

Instructors with a high orientation toward research tend also to show a high concern for students. Understandable because of their university orientation, they tend more than their colleagues to see the important ends of a two-year college education as an understanding and mastery of some academic discipline, preparation for further formal education, and aesthetic awareness. They would like to see more humanities courses required for students in occupational programs and more extracurricular colloquiums and seminars, exhibits, and recitals. And they would prefer more interdisciplinary courses.

The instructors who are oriented to research are an involved group. They participate in activities related to the humanities on their own time and attend classes, lectures, and seminars for their own benefit. They are high in "functional potential," "the university as a reference group," and "preference for further preparation." And, with it all, they have an extremely high orientation toward their students and their teaching—"research orientation" and "curriculum and instruction" showed one of the highest correlations of any pair of constructs. There is no support for the contention that an instructor's orientation toward research interferes with his teaching. On the contrary, the two may be mutually supportive.

CHAPTER

9

WHO NEEDS A
FULL-TIME
FACULTY?

In recent years collective bargaining for faculty members has received widespread attention. Numerous speculations have been made about its effect on faculty satisfaction and working conditions. Similarly, affirmative action has been argued: why it should or should not be implemented, its meaning for quality education and social justice. But for all the publicity, both these developments pale in their effect on the faculty when compared with the phenomenal rise in the employment of part-timers.

The figures tell the story. Although the data in Table 6, taken from the American Association of Community and Junior Colleges *Directory*, include

TABLE 6

Full- and Part-Time Two-Year College Instructors

Year	Total Faculty	Full-Time	Percent	Part-Time	Percent
1971	122,297	73,725	60	48,572	40
1972	129,889	76,796	59	53,093	41
1973	151,947	89,958	59	61,989	41
1974	162,530	81,658	50	80,872	50
1975	181,549	84,851	47	96,698	53

Source: American Association of Community and Junior Colleges, *Faculty in Two-Year Colleges* (Washington, D.C.: American Association of Community and Junior Colleges, 1975).

both full-time faculty teaching overload courses (usually in the evening) and people teaching less than a full complement of courses, they show the steady decline in percent of full-timers. The figures for the states with the largest community college systems are even more dramatic. In 1970 Illinois part-time faculty were 52 percent of the whole; in 1974 they numbered 63 percent. The part-time faculty in Florida increased 78 percent between 1970 and 1974, a time when the number of full-timers was *decreasing* by 8 percent. Of 34,300 California faculty in 1975, there were 14,273 full-time and 20,027 part-time. These numbers refer only to part-time faculty with no other institutional responsibilities. They do not include full-time instructors teaching an overload in the same institution.

The reasons for the rapid increase in employment of part-timers are easily discerned—changing college emphases and finances. The part that money plays is readily apparent—part-time faculty paid on hourly rate typically receive from one-third to one-half of the salary paid full-timers who teach an equivalent number of courses. Institutional funding is tied to student attendance; the same monies flow into the college whether the students are taught by full-timers or by part-timers. Both groups are comprised of fully licensed instructors; ostensibly the instruction delivered is the same and the funds received are the same.

Administrators know part-timers perform few of the services that the full-timers do in addition to meeting classes, but they are usually willing to forego the additional duties for the savings stemming from the salary differential. The part-timers, in effect, generate a profit for the college when they teach classes that would otherwise require the services of a full-time instructor. A bill introduced in the California Assembly in 1976 (A.B. 4430) puts it plainly: "Statewide part-timers in our community colleges bring in 40 percent of the average daily attendance, yet receive only 20 percent of the salaries, and therefore are subsidizing the operation of the colleges and their other employees" (pp. 4–5).

The protean emphases in community colleges are the second major reason for the explosive rise in utilization of part-time faculty. The argument runs as follows: community colleges serve best if they can develop new programs rapidly for new clientele. When the colleges were seen as the first two years of a baccalaureate sequence they employed academicians. When they moved strongly into occupational training they employed people with experience in the trades. But the rapid expansion of the 1950s and 1960s saw the colleges enrolling sizable percentages of students who did not want typical occupational or academic programs; many came for personal enrichment, others for leisure, others for basic or remedial education. At the colleges they met traditional faculty teaching traditional subjects. The long-standing tradition of academic freedom coupled with the basic resistance to change exhibited by most instructors handicapped the institution's ability to build programs for the new clients. Since the faculty would not or could not modify their instructional forms and curriculum patterns rapidly enough, the colleges were forced to employ a new group of instructors.

Yet at the same time the institutions did not want to get caught with a staff with nothing to do. Each time a full-time instructor is employed, the implication is that he will be with the college until he retires. The rapidly shifting curriculum patterns mean that the person would have to be retrained or otherwise encouraged to change his mode of teaching several times through his life. Since this proves difficult to effect, college administrators felt that employing part-timers who have little claim on the jobs would take care of the problem. As they put it, "When the part-time relatively uncommitted students wash away this time, we can wash out the part-time uncommitted faculty along with them."

Both these developments have changed the two-year college environment. Although part-time faculty hold the same teaching licenses as the full-timers, they occupy a completely different status within the institution. Beginning with the initial employment process and going through their perquisites; time spent on campus; relations with students, colleagues, and administrators; and on up to the severance process, nothing is quite the same. Faculty screening committees and the administrator interview process is not done as carefully for the part-timers as it is for the full-timers, the thinking being that since the part-timers will only be at the institution a short time there is no need to spend a great deal of time and money in selection. Affirmative action guidelines may be shaded—in many colleges the ethnic and sex compositions of the part-time faculty matches that of the full-timers, who were employed in years prior to affirmative action orders, suggesting that the orders have had little effect.

Evaluation, development, fringe benefits, support services—all are different for the part-timers. The California Community and Junior College Association (CCJCA) report on part-time faculty in California community colleges (Sewell, 1976) found that a sizable minority of the colleges have no evaluation policy for part-time faculty, while most those that do, use different procedures for the part-timers and the full-timers. Only one-half as many of the California colleges conduct in-service faculty development programs for part-timers as compared with those conducted for full-timers. Three-fourths of the colleges fail to provide office space for part-time instructors, even though most of them make clerical help available to them. The differences in treatment of part-timers and full-timers were summarized by Marsh and Lamb (1975), who found that at the extreme, the part-timers tend not to be evaluated as the full-timers, do not participate in faculty development, have little contact with students outside class, and have practically no contact with their peers.

What then has changed? If the part-time faculty are as qualified as the regular staff, the students, the programs, and the college itself should not suffer unless the part-timer's out-of-class responsibilities can be shown to be important. No one has yet demonstrated the value of committee service, maintaining office hours, collegial interaction in course planning, or continuity of instructor from one term to another. Lacking these data, we fall back on reviewing the part-timers' qualifications.

Defining the category, "part-time faculty members" is the first step. There is no uniform definition. The California Education Code defines them as people employed to teach not more than 60 percent of the hours constituting a full-time assignment. Elsewhere, in contractual agreements and college policies, they may be people teaching fewer than some number of hours per week or some fraction of the average load of full-time faculty in respective departments. In the Faculty Survey the part-timers were simply defined as those responding negatively to the question, "Are you considered to be a full-time faculty member?"

The survey sampling procedure yielded 70 percent full-timers, 30 percent part-timers. Some of the part-timers may have been missed for any of several reasons: many courses in the class schedules were listed as being taught by "staff," hence there was no name to pull for the survey; the sample was taken from the spring quarter class schedule when there are typically fewer courses, hence fewer part-timers employed; the sample was slightly weighted toward chairpersons who, of course, would not be part-timers; and the ratio of humanities courses is much smaller in the evening division than it is during the regular session. Counting the total faculty listed in the schedules, 20 percent of the full-timers teach in the humanities, whereas only 11 percent of the total part-time faculty is in the humanities. These figures have been confirmed in other studies; the CCJCA survey (Sewell, 1976) found the highest concentration of part-time instructors in business and management, public affairs and services, home economics, apprenticeships, computer and information science, and law. The humanities typically were taught by full-time instructors: 67 percent of the full-time equivalent in fine and applied arts; 65 percent in foreign language; 76 percent in letters.

The Faculty Survey found the humanities part-timers differentially represented in the various disciplines. The highest proportion of part-timers were in religious studies, foreign languages, and art. This is probably because a local minister might teach religious studies part-time at the college; English as a second language is frequently taught by teachers from local high schools; and local artists may do a section in art history or art appreciation at a college that cannot maintain a full-time person in that area. Further, instructors in these three fields might find more difficulty in teaching in a different area than would, for example, a history teacher assigned to political science. It is not as easy for one person in religious studies, foreign languages, or art in the smaller colleges to put together a full array of courses.

The institutional distribution of the part-time faculty differs, too. Colleges in the south tend to be heavily weighted toward full-time faculty members, whereas the large western institutions employ the greatest percentages of part-timers. The numbers for the west are dominated by California, where utilization of part-timers has been most heavy; in fact, in 1973 the full-time faculty increased by only 35 people, whereas more than 2,500 additional part-time faculty were employed. Nationwide the larger colleges—5,000 students and up— have the highest percentages of part-time instructors.

The part-timers come from many sources. About one-third of them had no employment other than at the college. A few seem to be retired people teaching one or two courses. Many are young people trying to get into full-time teaching at the same time that they complete their graduate studies at a nearby university, a point confirmed by the fact that nearly half the part-timers are age 35 or younger. Local high school teachers and business and professional people probably make up a sizable proportion of those who do have other jobs. Still another group is probably comprised of people who are teaching part-time at two or more institutions, commuting among them but not maintaining full-time responsibilities at any college.

Several differences between full-timers and part-timers appeared in the Faculty Survey. The part-time instructors are less experienced. The experience mode is one to two years for part-timers; five to ten years for the full-time faculty. Similarly the part-timers have taught fewer years in their current institution; 57 percent have been there two years or less, whereas only 20 percent of the full-timers fall into that category. The part-timers are less committed to the institution—51 percent of them would find a position at a four-year college "very attractive" whereas only 35 percent of the full-timers so indicated. Thirty-eight percent of the part-timers would find a position at another community or junior college "very attractive" as compared with only 15 percent of the full-timers. And they tend more to hold the university as a reference group.

The part-timers' qualifications differ also: 12 percent of them hold the doctorate, whereas 15 percent of the full-timers do. Full-timers are more likely to be working on doctorate degrees: 26 percent versus 18 percent of the part-timers. However, 16 percent of the part-timers are working on their master's; only 4 percent of the full-time humanities faculty are working on that degree. The part-timers' "preference for further preparation" is higher as well.

Although part-timers rank in the same order as full-timers the eight groups indicated on the Faculty Survey as sources of advice on teaching, they tend to rank colleagues somewhat less strongly. Their percentage responses as "quite useful" are higher for the remaining seven reference groups—nearly double in support of high school teachers.

All positions other than at the college look better to the part-timers. With the exception of "Doing what I'm doing now," more part-timers than full-timers rank all alternatives as "very attractive." Fifty-one percent of the part-timers as compared with 35 percent of the full-timers rank as "very attractive" a faculty position at a four-year college or university; and 38 percent of the part-timers compared with 15 percent of the full-timers a faculty position at another community or junior college.

Several questions in the survey attempted to ascertain the level of professional commitment. Here the part-timers were seen to be considerably lower. They read fewer scholarly journals and practically no professional education journals. They are less likely than the full-timers to be a member of a professional association, less concerned with research, less committed to curriculum and instruction, and less concerned with the humanities.

Nevertheless their concern for students shows up as being much the same as full-timers. As their full-time counterparts, part-timers think that self-knowledge and a sense of personal identity are the top most important qualities that a student should gain from a two-year college experience. Both groups also rank as least important of the six possible choices "an understanding/mastery of some academic discipline." Differences pertain, however, when it comes to other alternatives. In descending order, part-timers rank as "very important" preparation for further formal education, knowledge and skills directly applicable to careers, knowledge and interest in community and world problems, and aesthetic awareness. On the other hand, full-timers rank community awareness, preparation for further education, aesthetic awareness, and career skills.

Both groups select six and then four humanities courses as the number two-year college occupational students should be required to take, but more of the full-timers favor six or more, and more of the part-timers would opt for four. As far as noncurricular offerings are concerned, more full-timers than part-timers see a deficit in the number of colloquiums, lectures, exhibits, concerns, and films. Full-timers also claim to experience the humanities by attending exhibits/museums/shows, reading, listening to records and television, and talking with peers/associates more than their part-time colleagues. As for changes they would like to see in the humanities, both groups favor first the addition and improvement of humanities courses. But almost two to one, the full-timers favor integrating the humanities into interdisciplinary courses and more extracurricular courses.

Our measure of group affiliation or group cohesion is much the same for both samples—both related most to friends and least to college administrators. In descending order, they then rank family, other instructors in their field, most instructors at their school, students, and teacher organizations. Not unexpectedly, part-timers tend to be less related to other instructors in their field, most instructors in their school, and teacher organizations. While their relationship to friends is the same as the full-timers, they are more related to their families and, most interestingly, slightly more related to their students for this projective measure.

Their level of satisfaction, the ways they spend their free time, and the types of training they would prefer, are also the same. Considering that the part-timers are paid less and have little security of employment, the finding that their levels of satisfaction are no different from the full-timers is surprising. Satisfaction seems to be a personality trait qualitatively unrelated to external conditions.

But in terms of "functional potential," our measure of ego strength, part-timers are slightly below full-timers. Similarly, more part-timers are less involved in curriculum and instruction, less concerned with the humanities, and less concerned with students. Part-timers tend more to see the university as their reference group and to prefer further preparation.

Part-timers are different, but are the differences inportant? Does it matter that the full-timers have greater orientation to research, higher concern for curriculum and instruction, more concern for the humanities, and so on? Employers do not typically give an 11-page questionnaire to applicants; hence, they would not be aware of many of the differences that appeared in the Faculty Survey. If they were aware of these differences, there is little reason to believe they would modify their employment practices. The question of who gets hired turns not on the similarities or differences between full-time and part-time faculty but on matters totally unrelated to background, experience, and commitment to the profession. As long as the part-timers meet their classes, get their grades in on time, and avert student disaffection, district governing boards and administrators seem well satisfied.

Changes in employment practices would undoubtedly be stimulated if the difference in pay for full-time and part-time faculty teaching the same number and kind of classes were reduced. The pay scales are tending to move closer together. Pressure for pro-rata wages—equal pay for equal work—stem from both full-time faculty associations and their counterparts among part-timers. The full-timers want pro-rata wages so their own overload teaching receives higher pay and so the districts will tend to hire fewer part-timers, who have the effect of weakening the full-timers' bargaining position. The part-time faculty, banding together in associations of their own, want pro-rata pay for the obvious reason that it would increase their wages considerably. The college districts are not rushing toward pro-rata wage scales because of the increased costs and the concommitant reduced services (if marginally supported classes now taught by hourly rate instructors had to be canceled).

It is difficult to ascertain what a move to pro-rata pay for part-time faculty would cost. Comparisons are tenuous because full-time instructors are paid on a monthly or annual salary basis, while part-timers are usually paid on the number of hours they teach. Further, district policies and contracts covering full-time faculty members differ in terms of the minimum number of hours and duties other than classroom teaching that are required. Some contracts and policies specify instructors' maintaining office hours, committee assignments, student advising outside of class, and similar duties. Estimating full-timers' hourly compensation must include these other-than-classroom responsibilities. But regardless of the formulas applied, pro-rata pay would cost more.

Attempts have been made to pro-rate hourly pay on the number of hours full-timers work per week using various modal numbers. The Sewell study calculates hourly rates on 15-, 30-, and 40-hour weeks. Assuming a median full-time faculty salary to be $18,000 per year and 36 weeks a typical annual work time, at 15 hours work per week, the hourly salary is $33; at 30 hours per week, the rate would be $16.50; and at 40 hours per week, the rate would be $12.50. Calculating the full-time workweek at 40 hours, then, and assuming that part-time instructors *do nothing* other than meet their classes, the part-timers are adequately recompensed at current hourly rates.

Marsh and Lamb (1975) point up the difficulty in attempting to equate part-time and full-time teaching loads, concluding that the "comparable load" basis is most equitable. This method computes pro-rata pay using the part-timers' hours in class as related to the number of hours spent in class by full-timers in his particular teaching area. Accordingly, a part-time English instructor would be related only to the full-time English instructors, a part-time nursing instructor to the full-time nursing instructors, and so on. The number of hours that the full-timers spend in class and in preparing for class would be considered the base point from which the part-timer would derive his working load and salary. Thus, if an instructor were teaching 15 class hours per week, and assuming two hours of class preparation for each hour in class, he would have a total of 45 hours for that portion of his job. Assuming that extrainstructional duties are no more than one-fourth of the job, a total 60-hour week can be postulated. A part-timer teaching for six hours with no responsibilities other than classroom preparation, then, would be considered to be an 18-hour-a-week employee. Since 18 hours is 30 percent of 60, the part-timer teaching two classes would receive 30 percent of a full-timer's salary. On an $18,000 full-time salary (the median for 1974–75 in California) the part-timer would receive $5,400 for his two classes for each of two semesters, or $1,350 per class. This would be a considerable increase over the hourly rate, which at the time the data were assembled, averaged $12.50 per hour, or $675 for a three-hour course taught in an 18-week term. In short the pro-rata pay formula would double the part-timers' pay by, in effect, adding in the preparation time for which the full-timer is recompensed.

Regardless of the formula that is applied, any type of pro-rata pay would certainly increase the salary awarded to those part-timers now laboring under hourly rate agreements. Many community college districts have already adopted pro-rata pay for part-timers, and the trend is certainly in that direction. The fact remains, however, that in large measure the rapid community college expansion of recent years—particularly in the nontraditional program areas—has been supported by money saved through paying part-timers on an hourly rate. As this practice diminishes the colleges will be forced to retrench or to find additional funds elsewhere.

The trend toward employing increasingly large numbers of part-timers may also be reversed if community college enrollments decline. Because the part-timers have no job security they are the first to go. If for any reason the colleges curtail courses, the full-time faculty will most assuredly be retained to keep those that are left.

The full-timers themselves may force a reduction in the number of part-time employees. A strong union, for example, could negotiate for an absolute ratio between full-time and part-time staff, thus increasing jobs for prospective union members. Another circumstance—possible, but the least likely of all—is that the full-time faculty would convince the governing boards that they are worth the difference in pay. More likely is that the full-timers will move into a position of supervision of part-time instructors.

The question of part-time faculty employment can be examined from a standpoint other than its effects on college finances and individual faculty welfare. The issue is grounded in educational philosophy and institutional mission. For decades social philosophers have dreamed of the instantly responsive institution taking on educational needs as they appear. This institution would have no vested interests, no staff with favored areas that must be accommodated, but would offer just what its clients wanted.

The community college, with its sizable coterie of part-time instructors coming and going as educational needs appear, would seem to approximate this dream. Indeed, the tendency might be worthy if it were fully realized. But several questions remain unanswered: who decides what a community educational need is? How often are genuine community needs surveys run and acted upon? Is there sufficient intelligence among institutional managers to maintain institutional responsiveness? To what extent is curriculum formulation a process of accommodation to pressure groups? Are programs offered for a special clientele really easier to close when the faculty have no job security?

Even more broadly the question of part-time employment turns on the desirability of an educational community as opposed to a labile institution. The idea of an educational community seems to demand relatively permanent scholars presenting to the community a picture of a group with vision. At best the scholars assess the community, work with it, teach its young, interpret its goals. At worst they become reclusive and further their own interests.

The current trend seems toward an institution managed by professionals responding to what *they* perceive to be community needs. These needs are frequently areas for which the clients are willing to commit time and, through their taxes, funds; in short, almost completely a response to the marketplace. The seeming alternative to professional management is for the voters to elect state representatives who appoint state boards, which fund desired programs. This seems a long way around. If the faculty are not competent to judge program desirability, can legislatures, governing boards, and administrators necessarily display better vision? In sum, can we have an educational community when most of its staff are not institutionally integral to the system or professionally commited to teaching? On the other hand, can we have an instantly reponsive institution managed by nonacademic personnel responding to a plethora of conflicting signals?

The question will not be answered by educational philosophers—it is rarely asked—but by those in the political arena. The various part-timers associations that have been formed in recent years petition for pro-rata pay, space, aides, year-long contracts (as opposed to semester-long), and due process in separation from the institution. Their argument is for one class of instructors, fully qualified and recompensed. Some of the major professional associations have recommended that employment, evaluation, compensation, and staff development for part-timers be more closely brought in line with the existing policies for the full-time instructional staff. Still the questions remain: if the part-timers had fully equivalent status and professional commitment, would the instantly responsive college be enhanced, reduced, or remain the same? Does responsibility for the level of responsiveness lie with the full-time faculty? With the administrators? The board members? Or, is the educational community an archaism never to be seen apart from the residential liberal arts colleges of late memory?

CHAPTER
10

FACULTY DEVELOPMENT
AND PREPARATION

It is difficult to separate faculty development from faculty preparation. Development pertains to the maturation of the individual, his cognitive, affective, and social growth as a person and as a practitioner. Preparation is a narrower term typically used for the experiences structured for an individual as he develops prior to, or within, the profession. The terms are frequently used interchangeably along with other terms such as training or renewal for any activity that has the intention of changing the way instructors conduct their work or feel about their work situation.

As a concept, faculty development has received much attention recently in the universities as well as in the two-year colleges. The universities have become concerned with it because of some of the charges that have been leveled at them. During the 1960s, when research funds were readily available and vigorously pursued by university faculty members, the institutions were admonished for their impersonality by their own students and by other critics. Community college spokesmen did not shrink from the opportunity to castigate the universities while lauding their own colleges as "teaching institutions." However, under the impact of reduced funds for research, and because of their own need to compete for students, the universities have tended to become more responsive to student demands for personable instructors and worthwhile courses. Accordingly, even the major research universities have instituted faculty preparation programs for their own staff that turn the instructors' attention to the importance of teaching. In fact, many universities seem to have made a distinct shift away from demanding public subsidies for scholarship and research and have looked toward the marketplace, offering their students pleasurable experiences of immediate utility through good teachers and good courses. The literature of higher education reflects this shift of emphasis. Much of the work emanating from the Wright Institute in Berkeley, California, has dealt with faculty development. Many writers have suggested that universities must pursue faculty development because student development is hampered if the students are confronted with poorly developed instructors who wish they were doing something other than teaching. Students see themselves as consumers of education who deserve delivery on promises. Taxpayers demand accountability on the part of the institution. All these contentions can be summarized as follows: the students new to higher education who come from other than the traditional college-going population need to be taught because they are limited in their ability to study and learn by themselves; the scholarly reputation of the faculty is not necessarily related to the quality of undergraduate instruction and, indeed, may constitute a barrier to good teaching; faculty development is as important for the professor with a good reputation as a scholar as it is for the neophyte; it is difficult to get people to change the way they have been conducting their work for all of their professional life.

Gaff (1975) takes the position that with few new faculty being hired in universities, the institutions will have to rely on their current professors to provide new ideas in instruction and leadership for innovative teaching programs. Along with most other commentators on teaching in the university, Gaff suggests that the improvement of instruction must be the focus of faculty development activities, that faculty must be helped to develop greater competence in their teaching and a more professional approach to education.

Most university-based faculty development programs are designed to assist the faculty in exploring their attitudes about teaching and learning, acquiring more knowledge about professional education, enhancing their sensitivities to students and colleagues, developing teaching skills, and understanding how they can balance the teaching role with their other professional responsibilities. Here the programs merge professional competence with personal growth and where they do, they may be based on both psychological and instructional principles. Nonetheless, the programs that are labeled faculty development are not always so constructed. A national survey conducted by Many, Ellis, and Abrams (1972) indicates that although over half the responding institutions reported the existence of in-service faculty development programs, most of them were relatively casual, enjoying little budgetary support. Most had to do with teaching new instructional forms.

Since 1970 numerous additional university-based centers for teaching and learning have been opened. More than 200 of these centers are listed in *Toward Faculty Renewal* (Gaff, 1975). Most serve as programs for faculty development in the broader sense, turning the faculty's attention to undergraduate instruction, relating tips on teaching and techniques for student assessment along with attempting to change basic attitudes toward the profession. At the University of California the variously named offices of instructional development attempt to increase faculty awareness of instructional alternatives. The university has further made a distinct effort to infuse the process attendant to advancing a faculty member in rank with information about the professor's effectiveness with his students.

The teaching imperative has been felt in the university to the extent that many respected scholars make pleas for supervised teaching experiences for all neophyte instructors. Riesman (1975) recognizes the additional cost that must be borne by graduate students in prolonging their studies through supervised teaching assignments, but he maintains that they must do so to attend to the necessary activities of teaching, the profession in which they will be engaged.

Because the community college faculty have typically not been concerned with research, the need for instructional development centers seems not as pronounced as at the university. Nevertheless, two-year colleges have been faced with changing conditions that have led them, too, toward the development of faculty renewal programs. The most pronounced of these conditions is the reduction in growth of new full-time staff members. When the community colleges were expanding rapidly the phenomenon of growth itself was covered, occasioned by inadequate staff members. But as the growth slowed and college leaders realized that an uncaring or incompetent instructor was theirs to keep until he retired, the call for faculty development came to the fore.

The new educational programs designed to serve the new types of students in community colleges provided another impetus for faculty development. As the institutions moved from basic reliance on college parallel and occupational programs to compensatory education and numerous other forms of nontraditional studies, the need for faculty to be retrained became apparent. And as the colleges began attracting ever-increasing numbers of ethnic minority group members, the plaint that traditional faculty could not teach these students became widely heard.

Court decisions holding that instructors could not be readily dismissed provided yet a third reason for in-service staff development in two-year colleges. The courts have held generally that an instructor may not be dismissed for incompetence unless the institution has shown how it had attempted to assist the instructor to correct his deficiencies. These rulings have been interpreted to mean that the college must have a distinctly identifiable program of staff development.

The faculty development programs that have been built have centered on attitude adjustment—accepting the basic concepts of the community college and the types of students as one's own—and on innovative modes of instruction. At their best the programs allow individual instructors to test instructional strategies, assess their own goals, and measure their personal and professional development. They may also tend to change the campus climate in the direction of support for the individual. At their worst, the programs take the form of pedantic seminars or hortatory declamations designed to inspire people to change their outlook, lifestyle, and mode of professional functioning all in one hour. Where there is no consistency or focus, the faculty development effort falls on stony ground. The faculty may go along with the fiction, though, if their college's staff development efforts translate into funds for sabbatical leaves and travel to professional meetings in distant cities.

The recent flurry of interest in faculty renewal may lead to better programs, but there is no consensus on how it should be done. Faculty renewal programs suffer from identification with in-service training, a catch-all term for activities conducted by the college that were presumed to have an effect on an instructor's professional functioning. Over the years in-service training has included college-sponsored workshops, instructional development grants, faculty retreats, preschool orientation meetings, small group meetings with administrators, and numerous other forms. It was never a high priority item, and it tended to fall into disrepute because there was no way to evaluate its effect and because the instructors themselves felt left out of the process of planning the exercises. If outside speakers are to be called in, the instructors want to say who shall be invited. And if workshops are to be conducted, they want them to be concerned with problems of their own discipline.

To be successful, in-service faculty preparation programs must be supported enthusiastically by the faculty. One popular technique is an exchange program, wherein an instructor is sent to another college for a term and his replacement is an instructor from that college. It allows the faculty to perceive working in a different milieu and, whether or not it changes long term behavior, it does affect personal satisfaction. Workshops in an academic discipline are also usually enthusiastically received, especially if they are conducted by instructors from other two-year colleges. The Education Professions Development Act sponsored numerous projects open to two-year college faculty members, and the National Science Foundation similarly funded cooperative workshops organized around the disciplines in the sciences. These tended to be most successful where the two-year college staff was involved in the planning and conduct of the workshops themselves.

Colleges sometimes participate jointly in staff development. A faculty member from each of 18 Alabama two-year colleges participated in a summer program designed to teach him how to become a faculty development training agent at his own college (Preus and Williams, 1975). Following the session, the instructors returned to their campuses to implement programs for their colleagues, trying various forms of meetings, teaching modules, and communication links for the purpose of leading faculty toward innovative instruction and student evaluation processes. Although program participants tended to form more positive attitudes toward community college concepts during the year that the in-service programs were operative, little more resulted. The major effect of the program seemed to be that the trainers themselves benefited most. The planners concluded that there should have been more care exercised in selecting the on-campus trainers, more funding or more limited program scope, more than one training agent for each participating college, and a requirement that each agent form program strategies that would include specific measurable results. One of the bright spots of the program was the fact that they included an evaluation component.

Summer workshops have also been organized under the auspices of other agencies. The Danforth Foundation conducted a series of popular summer institutes in which teams of administrators, counselors, board members, students, and instructors from colleges were invited to work on problems peculiar to their institutions. The National Endowment for the Humanities has also arranged summer workshops in nearly all disciplines in the humanities as well as providing fellowships for year-long studies in some areas.

Year-long institutes, short term workshops, staff retreats, seminar series, encounter groups, packaged programs, and numerous short term visits, meetings, and conventions have also been tried. Many of the types of staff development activities have been summarized by O'Banion (1973) from the standpoint of the institution that needs an alert, innovative, ever-aware staff if it is best to serve its students. Our own work (Cohen and Brawer, 1972a) starts from the position that the instructor must develop both personally and professionally if he is to work toward that period of actualization that is true maturity. Whether institutional or personal, faculty development is—or should be—an issue of high priority in the colleges.

The universities continue to play a role in both preservice and in-service education of community college faculty. Instructors in academic fields are required to hold university-awarded credentials, and most college salary schedules are still arrayed with increments for additional credits and degrees earned in graduate school. Nonetheless, the uncoordinated accumulation of university credits has been criticized as failing to enhance faculty development and especially for failing to effect greater faculty commitment to community college goals. Moreover, the concept of faculty development as an individual growth process typically gets lost in preservice preparation. The usual preparation program is based on academic subject matter. The instructor learns history or English or nursing and then is released to teach it. Because of the nature of universities, the programs center on awarding degrees certifying knowledge about that subject. The extent to which the degree guarantees the ability to teach the subject, to transmit his knowledge, is another matter. Nonetheless, because the degree is accepted as the credential for purposes of salary employment, the preservice programs survive.

Criticism of university-based preparation programs has been widespread. Those community college advocates who are concerned with their institutions' efforts in teaching members of minority groups assail the university for failing to make special provisions within their credentials programs for members of these groups. They say that minority group students need minority group teachers both as models and because the teachers are more likely to empathize with students. The commentators who are concerned with the community college's role in compensatory education complain that subject area master's degree programs offer nothing of use to the person who will have to teach in remedial or developmental programs. Those who are concerned with innovative curriculum development aver that the graduate school-based programs train teachers in too narrow a segment of the subject area. They want preparation programs that span across several academic departments. And those who want the community college supported for its role in community development condemn all training that deals with subject matter of any stripe. They want people who will understand the community colleges' mission and be able to work directly in the social and political processes of the community through their community service and community outreach programs.

The university's response has been slow. The subject matter master's remains the dominant form of preservice preparation. Many graduate schools of education teach courses in the junior college and offer supervised teaching experiences in two-year colleges. But in all cases only a minority of those students obtaining master's degrees in academic departments participate in those courses and experiences. Occasionally a special master's degree program for two-year college instructors will be organized in an academic department with or without the intervention of the school of education. The program may well include an internship in a local two-year institution but most departments depend on teaching assistantships in their own undergraduate programs for training their graduates in pedagogy.

Still, there have been some modifications. The fact that the community college holds the greatest potential for employing graduates of programs in English has led to many revisions in that field. The master's degree program in English at numerous institutions includes not only the traditional courses but also an internship at a local secondary school or community college and correlative work in other departments. Hill (1972) recommended that teacher preparation for philosophers include not only the teaching assistantship, which he saw as not greatly beneficial, but also a community college internship. The value of exchange programs between two- and four-year college faculties was also noted. Foreign language instructors are urged to participate in programs in area studies so they can teach the social, political, and historical identity of speakers of a particular language as well as teaching the language itself.

Numerous other revisions in master's degree programs might be mentioned, but the fact remains that the community college is changing so rapidly that it is difficult for graduate departments to keep up with the shifts. The reduction in employment of new instructors has cut down on the pressure for new graduate preservice programs; but, curiously, the reduction in the market for people with master's degrees is leading universities to make program modifications to make their graduates more marketable. In the 1960s, when two-year colleges were employing master's degree holders in wholesale lots, the universities were less responsive to cries for modified preparation sequences. Their people were being hired anyway. In the 1970s they have been forced to attempt to make their products more attractive.

There has been a shift, too, in the two-year colleges' pronouncements of the competence of their faculties. When they were concerned most with breaking away from the high school image they pointed with pride to the number of faculty with master's degrees, saying that students were more likely to meet faculty with higher degrees in the community colleges than they were in the universities, where they were frequently taught by teaching assistants. But after the severance with the high school was complete, they began speaking of faculty who better understood the various types of students with whom they were confronted. The community college spokesman who now recounts the value of his faculty talks about the way they relate to students, not to academic disciplines.

Nonetheless, the degree still holds an aura; many people still want it. In the Faculty Survey a construct, "preference for further preparation" was erected to differentiate among people who might want more additional preparation. Such questions as, "Would you like to take steps toward professional development in the next five years?" and "If you had a free summer, what would you do with it?", were asked. The construct did not differentiate well because 86 percent of the respondents said they would like some form of preparation; however, some differences among them may be noted.

More people teaching foreign languages, history, and political science are in the high "preference for further preparation" group than the low, whereas teachers of liberal arts, literature, and music tend toward the low group. Those who hold their highest degrees in foreign language tend slightly toward the low group, as do education and literature majors. More people with majors in history and political science tend toward the high group. Somewhat more instructors who had themselves been students in community/junior colleges tend toward the low "preference for further preparation" group. More males tend to be in the high group, more females in the low.

Although age differences relating to other variables have not been consistent, a pattern does emerge for the construct "preference for further preparation." Younger people and faculty members who are 61 or older are more desirous of further preparation, an interesting observation in terms of the older group. Faculty who had been instructors or administrators in secondary schools and those with four-year college or university experience tend generally toward the low group. New instructors are more inclined to want further preparation; full-time instructors are less likely to want it. The people desiring further preparation do not necessarily tend to read scholarly journals.

Considering positions that might be attractive five years hence, more people in the high than low "preference for further preparation" group would see as very attractive a faculty position at a four-year college or university, a faculty position at another two-year college, an administrative position in a community or junior college, and, to a lesser degree, a school outside the United States. More people in the low group would see as very attractive the continuation of their present activities. Further, if they were to begin all over again, the type of training they would seek also separates the low and high populations. More people in the low group would do the same—change nothing or study humanities.

Also distinguishing between high and low groups is the manner of experiencing the humanities beyond teaching. More lows tend to visit art museums; attend shows, exhibits, concerts, or theater; read; listen to records and television or radio; and participate in theater groups. More highs attend classes, lectures, or seminars. More people in the high group would like to see their colleges add and improve humanities courses as well as offer more extracurricular courses.

Both highs and lows rate affiliations with other groups in much the same manner, but the people low in "preference for further preparation" tend to be somewhat less related to these groups. The biggest contrast here is in terms of students; people in the high "preference for further preparation" group tend more to be affiliated with students.

Instructors who desire more preparation are well-integrated people, high in "functional potential." They are strongly oriented toward the university as a reference group and toward research. But they also rank high on "curriculum and instruction" and "concern for students." Preference for "further preparation" does not relate significantly with "satisfaction," nor with "concern with humanities."

Despite the furor regarding faculty development occasioned by demands for faculty accountability and evaluation, faculty development is not a high priority in the community college. Most districts allocate some funds to it, but these are often dissipated in weekend retreats, short term instructional development grants, faculty fellowships, leaves to do graduate study, and a host of uncoordinated experiences. Perhaps that is all that can be done in the absence of a consistently held perception of what the mature instructor should do and be. Nonetheless, we know enough about how people mature and develop to do better. And most of the concepts and practices in instruction are not so arcane that they cannot be taught readily. As with so many other aspects of two-year college leadership, faculty development depends on a vision of desired ends.

CHAPTER
11

DOES THE DOCTORATE
MAKE A DIFFERENCE?

During the 1960s, there were 60,000 new staff members employed in two-year colleges nationwide. During the 1980s, according to A. M. Cartter, fewer than 20,000 new faculty will be needed. This includes everyone necessary to replace people lost through death or retirement, and it accounts for new enrollments. Newly employed faculty members with doctorates will total between 2,650 and 3,960 of the 20,000, or from 13 to 20 percent of new hires. Accordingly, as Cartter put it, "The two-year college sector is not likely to represent a vast new untapped market for doctorates being trained by the nation's graduate schools" (Cartter and Salter, 1975, p. 40).

Cartter's interest was in a market for graduates with higher degrees, but his figures are useful for those concerned with the two-year college faculty. Will doctoral degree holders get hired in preference to others? Should they? If they do, will the two-year college faculty as a whole shift their emphasis and orientation?

The Faculty Survey shed some light on those questions. First, Cartter's estimate that from 13 to 20 percent of new hires will hold the doctorate may be high. According to the American Council on Education surveys of 1968–69 and 1972–73, newly employed faculty with doctorates numbered around 6 percent (Bayer, 1970; 1973). The total faculty in community colleges with doctorate degrees was less than 9 percent during those same years. Our survey found 14 percent of the full-timers with the doctorate (including doctors of divinity and doctors of jurisprudence). We are predicting that from 20 to 22 percent of the full-time degree-credit instructors in community colleges will have the doctorate by 1980. But this does not mean that 20 to 22 percent of the newly employed faculty will have it.

Most two-year college faculty members with a doctorate acquire it after years on the job; typically they do not enter the institution holding the degree.

This was confirmed in the Faculty Survey. More than one-third of the people with doctorates in the sample group were age 51 or greater, whereas fewer than one-fourth of the total sample were in the older age group. Further, 19 percent of the people teaching humanities hold their highest degree in education, suggesting that the person with a master's in a teaching discipline picks up a doctorate in education along the way.

Although a much higher percent of instructors in 1975 held the doctorate as compared with 1970 figures, the reason may be that the growth in faculty slowed considerably in the intervening years. Heretofore, faculty members who attained doctorates while they were on the job were offset by the influx of new people without higher degrees, thus maintaining a constant ratio of under 10 percent of the whole. Now that the percentage of new full-timers employed annually has dropped off considerably, the tendency of working faculty to obtain doctoral degrees has moved the overall percentage up. In the survey, 24 percent of the faculty without doctorates said they were currently working toward one. If only one-fourth of them complete this degree in the next five years, the 20 to 22 percent prediction will hold.

However, the data also show that some people fresh from graduate school are being employed. Doctorates are underrepresented in the middle age groups, but a high percent of them are quite young. The bimodal distribution of young and old instructors with doctorates applies also to the age of the colleges where they work. Older faculty with doctorates are predominantly in colleges established prior to 1960; younger ones tend to be in the colleges opened since 1970. Colleges organized in the 1960s, when there was a paucity of candidates from whom to select faculty, are less likely to have many faculty holding this advanced degree.

If many new colleges are organized in the 1980s, a sizable percentage of new doctorates may be employed. However, nothing suggests that the number of newly employed faculty with doctorates in older colleges will change. When division and department chairpersons were asked whether there was pressure to hire or not to hire people with the doctorate, fewer than 5 percent indicated pressure either way. In response to an open-ended question asking why they would or would not hire doctoral degree holders, most said, "We hire the best person regardless of the degree." Many chairpersons thing that the doctoral degree holders are "more capable and knowledgeable," but the administrators shy away from employing them because of the additional salary they command and because the degree is not necessary to teach in the college. Nevertheless, 61 percent of the chairpersons indicated they plan to hire instructors holding doctorates. As many said, "They are fine teachers," as said, "Their performance is the same as others."

Because most faculty with doctoral degrees have obtained them after years of teaching experience, they have been socialized to the college before—and often during—their graduate studies. Accordingly their attitudes toward the college and the teaching profession differ little from those held by their colleagues. However, there are some differences in career patterns. Doctoral degree holders are less likely to have had secondary school experience or to have been employed at another community college. They are more likely to be employed full-time, to have had four-year college experience, or experience as an administrator in a community college. More of them are males, and more see four-year college teaching or two-year college administration as desirable for themselves in the future. They are less likely to see teaching in another two-year college as a goal.

Doctoral degree holders also display a few characteristics that differentiate them from their colleagues. They are more likely to be members of professional associations, to attend meetings, and present papers. They read more journals and see their free time as being well spent in research and writing. They would have preferred more teaching methods courses in their own preparation but are less likely to want more professional development now.

They are different, too, in their view of students. They are less likely to see students as useful sources of advice on teaching, less likely to see the most important outcomes of college as self-knowledge or an understanding of an academic discipline. They run significantly lower on the construct, "concern for students." But they are more likely to see the benefits of career education for their students.

The doctoral holders see curriculum slightly differently. They would like more interdisciplinary courses, more seminars, and small group teaching. They are less likely to express a need for more extracurricular offerings of any type or for changes in humanities instruction. They are not different on the curriculum and instruction construct in terms of distribution of high, medium, and low groups.

Otherwise there are no differences. The doctoral degree holders are the same as the total group on "satisfaction," "functional potential," and "concern with humanities." They are somewhat overrepresented in the large colleges in the Middle Atlantic states, less in the midwest.

If people with doctorates are so little different from the rest of the faculty, why would a college employ them? The answer is simple—why not? It looks a little better to the accrediting commissions to have a few doctorates on the staff and brings a little prestige to the college among lay people and students. When placed against the total budget for personnel, the cost differential is slight. Many administrators feel that faculty members with scores of graduate units beyond the master's may well be better teachers. Although the Faculty Survey data do not support that contention, they certainly do not refute it.

A different question should be asked: Why do faculty want the degree? Here, again, a simple answer can be given. The doctorate brings prestige among one's colleagues and a feeling of personal accomplishment. Further, progression on the salary schedule in most two-year colleges is effectually automatic with people receiving increments according to their years of experience and graduate credits earned. Obtaining a doctorate almost invariably is rewarded with a salary increase of up to 20 percent above what one earns with a master's alone. It is important, too, for the instructor with aspirations toward administration. The type of doctorate, major field, or institution where it was earned matters little.

Some conclusions for graduate educators can be drawn. Community college administrators frequently say that graduate education is inadequate for teachers in their institutions. They want teachers with a community college "point of view," teachers who can work with all types of students. They want a flexible faculty, instructors who will plan courses carefully, use reproducible media, and, above all, accept students who are obviously nonscholars. They want faculty who do not hold a strict allegiance to a single academic discipline but those who are able and willing to teach in two or three fields.

The faculty have different concerns. They frequently object to currently offered degrees because of residence requirements, admissions criteria, involved application processes, and lack of proximity to jobs. They want courses offered on nights and Saturdays so they can obtain the degree with minimal effort while they sustain a full-time job. Lest this sound like an overstatement, consider the figures for the NOVA University National Ed.D. Program for Community Colleges. NOVA began its program in 1972 with the specific requirement that applicants have a job in a community college and be willing to work on the degree on occasional weekends during the year and for a few weeks during the summer. The program now has more than 800 two-year college practitioners enrolled. And NOVA is only one of many programs of the type. Do practitioners enroll in them because they stand to learn more from a more outstanding faculty than the traditional graduate schools can display? Or is it because the programs are offered as nonresident sequences that demand less commitment?

The university that seeks to build a doctoral degree program for community college instructors must take these assertions into account. Although only a few jobs will be available for new faculty members in coming years, a great many two-year college faculty members obtain doctorates. A program that allows them to do so while retaining their positions will succeed if it allows them to study in their home area at their own pace.

Specifically, a doctoral program for two-year college faculty should (1) serve commuters. It should be for faculty who are concurrent full-time or part-time employees in community college districts and who want a higher degree to learn more about the subject field, gain prestige within their institution, move higher on the salary schedule, or to increase their own sense of accomplishment. There will be few new full-time jobs available; hence, a program designed for students fresh from undergraduate programs would attract the wrong group. Short of natural attrition, there is literally no chance for people with higher degrees—no matter how well qualified—to replace faculty currently teaching in the colleges. The program must be available to people who cannot come to the university campus for extended periods of time; two-year college sabbatical leave policies are typically not generous.

The proposed program should (2) straddle departments where feasible. A doctorate in social sciences, humanities, or life sciences, rather than in psychology, theater history, or microbiology, would be better received. The number of interdisciplinary courses in community colleges is increasing. Even more to the point, many faculty teach in multiple subject areas. Many employing administrators tend to shun applicants with a strong affinity for a single academic discipline. Few community college faculty members read journals in their disciplines; they have little opportunity to stay abreast of developments in the field. A degree program that assists them in making interrelationships among disciplines is well suited for them.

The program must (3) offer classes, workshops, modules, and lectures on the community college campus itself. The faculty want and will subscribe overwhelmingly to a degree program that provides its courses on their campus. Traveling to a university is seen as unnecessary and undesirable. Any mode of information transmission offered on site is preferred.

The plan should (4) involve community college faculty members as clinical professors. They can set up the on-site workshops. The faculty like associating with their peers. They look forward to hearing from people teaching in their area who come from other colleges.

The administrator should (5) appoint a program head who will take responsibility for all aspects of the program. This must be someone who sees his role as recruiting students to the program, selecting courses within the university that fit the program, setting up new courses and on-site workshops, and counseling students. The program cannot be managed by a person who sees it as a subordinate responsibility.

Another factor to be included is (6) a teacher of teachers component. The program should assist two-year college division and department chairpersons to be supervisors and coordinators of curriculum and instruction. This allows for a leverage effect, getting the university more influence in the institution than it can obtain merely by training a few people a year within the various colleges.

Finally, the program should (7) serve functions other than to award degrees. Even though the program should rest on a coherent curriculum, it need not be limited to degree service. The workshops, special courses, and inter-institutional relationships established can be used as modules for upgrading faculty who already hold the doctorate. The incentives for enrollment are not there—most colleges have a ceiling on pay—but short courses on-site will attract a few of the professionally committed.

Some institutions have done this—successful programs have been established at the University of Michigan for two-year college teachers of English, and at Carnegie-Mellon University for social science and history instructors. There are others; but in many universities the graduate faculty has taken the position,

"Well, since many of our doctoral graduates cannot get first-choice positions in four-year colleges I suppose they will be going to community colleges. Therefore, we ought to modify our offerings a bit and teach them something about working in a two-year institution." Programs reflecting such parochial views deservedly attract few enrollees.

12

REFERENCE GROUP
IDENTIFICATION

In *Don't Smile Until Christmas*, K. Ryan quotes an insightful teacher who looks back on her first year of teaching by remarking, "But I did not know myself nor . . . the role I haphazardly tried to play. . . . I could not seem to gain from imitating those whom I thought successful teachers. Teaching, I finally decided, is somehow too closely knit into the basic fabric of one's character and personality to be copied" (1970, pp. 105, 119).

The aphorism "know thyself" applies to teachers as well as to all others who would step beyond the mundane and strive for some degree of self-actualization. At the same time, a fair amount of maturity is necessary if a person is to divorce himself from the role models previously held and discover how best to function independently.

Reference groups actually provide a filter through which the individual looks at himself as well as at the people with whom he interacts—authority figures, friends, colleagues. The person perceiving the way he and his colleagues are viewed by others may well understand better his own orientation toward work. Sometimes these models or reference sources persist throughout life. Most of us—at whatever age—still cherish some idols; and although these may be gradually acquiring clay feet, they still are seen as a cut above one's everyday experiences with others. It is good to emulate in part, but better yet to respect, to integrate those characteristics one esteems into the woof and warp that is the essence of oneself and still achieve an individuality that is one's very own. Indeed, unless the person operates within his own framework, he is doomed to frustration. The most consistently unsuccessful instructor that we have ever encountered was a professor who "knew" that "good teachers must be permissive." For years, determined to manage his classes on a "Well, what do *you* think?" basis, he condemned himself to violent headaches and his students to anxious bewilderment. In the idiom of the 1970s, one must do his own thing.

Doing your own thing, however unique, is still dependent upon one's experience with significant others throughout his life span. Regardless of the ways one perceives these others, regardless of the way he addresses work or personal life, he is, to some extent, always influenced by them. The elementary teacher who inspired one's art work, the secondary teacher who acted as yearbook coordinator, the university professors who exposed one to disciplines and thoughts not previously known—all these become part of the person.

Nevertheless, although some form of integration between self and others is both inevitable and desirable, a concentration on others to the extent of losing a sense of self must be seen as negative. This pertains to education and teaching as much as to any other field—in some cases even more so, since everyone has had instructors who stand out in one way or another. In terms of the two-year colleges, it was especially apparent when faculty members came directly from positions as secondary school instructors. They tended to look to the high school teacher as their primary reference group; and although many strove to move away from this image, pervious patterns were too well established to make the transition to independence completely successful. This image of the two-year college being populated by former secondary school teachers persisted for some time and helped give rise to the once common description of the junior college as a high school with ashtrays.

Now, with the secondary school no longer the primary source of supplying faculty, with the new recruits to two-year college teaching for the most part coming directly from student status in the university or from the business world, the emphasis has shifted. In itself, this shift may also pose a threat to identity. Indeed, we have previously suggested that the two-year college instructor who is operating somewhere between secondary school teacher and university professor is in an ambivalent position—this uncertainty being reflected in and reflecting a lack of clarity of direction. Standing uneasily between two levels of education, holding orientations in common with both groups, the faculty are only beginning to carve out a defined place for themselves. They still prefer to see themselves as "college professors," even at the expense of their seeking to create a unique niche for themselves and their own institutions. In fact, many readily admit they would really rather teach in a four-year college or university than in the two-year college. Apparently, the university—or more accurately, the junior college instructor's perception of it—still carries a golden aura.

Identification with the university may be appropriate in some ways. The increase of university-type senates in community colleges demonstrates the instructors' increasing voice in institutional operations. The severe reduction—and in some states, the complete elimination—of credential requirements, establishes the ties between the two-year college and the university and four-year college even more closely than those between the two-year institution and the secondary school. These changes strengthen the image of instructors as college professors rather than as school teachers.

Yet, no matter how many aspects of the university may be discerned in the status and functioning of junior college instructors, these individuals must still be true to themselves. The nature of their responsibilities are different for several reasons, all of which relate to the two-year college's commitment to teaching. While, for example, the defined tasks of university faculty members include teaching, that act is actually subordinate to several of their other functions. On the other hand, the main purpose of two-year college instructors is to teach. University professors are concerned with a narrow disciplinary range, a specific segment of an area of knowledge. The two-year college teacher, however, must be committed to a broad field of teaching that often encompasses several disciplines. In the university, research is ostensibly for the purpose of gaining new knowledge. Whether conducted by instructors or by others, research in the two-year college is usually geared toward seeking better ways to help students learn. First and last, then, two-year colleges purport to be teaching institutions. For instructors in these colleges, the process of instruction is crucial to identity formation.

Recognizing one's debts to others while still maintaining a sense of individuality is a sign of maturity. It is also another way to understand the person. Thus, in the Faculty Survey that forms the basis for the data presented in this book, several items were included that provide information on role models. In addition, a coterie of items was included as the construct, "university as reference group." The construct is important because the way one conducts both his personal and professional life is in part, consciously or unconsciously, dependent on the role models he holds. Personal orientation would vary considerably, for example, if the most viable reference group were one's colleagues rather than one's university professors.

From responses to specific items as well as to the "university as reference group" construct, then, we find answers to such questions as: How do two-year college faculty members perceive others as role models? To whom do they look as sources of advice on teaching? What is the profile of instructors who are high in this construct? Who tend least to look at the university?

This chapter presents information about role models or reference groups. We deal here with specific relationships between the construct "university as reference group" and other pertinent variables.

A major way of determining an individual's reference group is to ask what he would like to be doing in the future. We presented the faculty with eight choices of positions that they would see as attractive or unattractive five years hence. The choice, "A faculty position at a four-year college or university," was seen as "very attractive" or "somewhat attractive" by 75 percent of the respondents. The choice, "I would be doing what I'm doing now," attracted positive responses from 78 percent of the group. All other choices ranked far below. In short, if the faculty see themselves as working anywhere other than in their current positions they perceive a move to the university as most attractive.

"An administrative position in a community or junior college" ranked high among division and department chairpersons, already quasi administrators, and a position in "a school outside the United States" received approval from 61 percent of the respondents.

These responses may best be interpreted through viewing them in terms of one's reference group. Although the faculty are most closely associated with their colleagues and their current positions and, hence, would be expected to perceive them with most favor, the idea of a university is about as appealing. The university pays little more on average, but it does maintain a position of enhanced status. Whether or not they are dissatisfied with their current lot the faculty view the university with esteem.

And yet, when asked to rate eight different groups in terms of their usefulness as sources of advice on teaching, university professors did not fare well. They ranked just ahead of programs of professional organizations, high school teachers, and administrators. Apparently, a university position is seen as desirable even though one does not expect that university professors know much about teaching, the primary activity for the community college instructor.

Other responses were integrated into the construct "university as reference group"; and the respondents were put into high, medium, and low categories according to their score at the mean or one standard deviation on either side of it.

A few differences pertain to people in the various disciplines in terms of this construct. The history faculty are notably overrepresented on the high end of the "university as reference group"; literature instructors tend more to be in the low group. As might be expected, the people with doctorates tend more to be in the high group. Males and females do not differ on this construct, but part-time instructors are more likely to be in the high group than are full-time instructors. This may be explained by the fact that many part-timers are graduate students or recent university graduates and might well be expected to continue to perceive the university with some favor. Similarly the humanities sample are more likely to be high on "university as reference group" than the people in other than humanities fields, many of which include occupational areas.

There is a strong relationship between length of service on the job and "university as reference group." People who have had more experience as instructors or administrators in two-year colleges are less likely to see the university as their reference group. Accordingly, the older instructors and those with more secondary school experience as well as those who have been in the community college for a number of years tend away from the university. This group includes more than its proportionate share of chairpersons who not only tend to be in the low end of the "university as reference group" division but also say that they do not plan to employ people with the doctorate.

Also consistent with expectation is the fact that the people who see the university as their reference group tend to read more scholarly journals and are more likely to want to take steps toward professional development. The data also seem to indicate that those in the high end of "university as reference group" have more of a professional identity than those on the other end. For example, they would like to take classes or do research, to study or write for publication, to work on an advanced degree if they had a free summer. The people on the low end suggest they would take the time off to rest or engage in recreational activities. Those in the high group are more involved in other ways; if they were to engage in preparatory training over again, they would do more student teaching, take more teaching methods courses, and get a higher degree.

The construct "university as reference group" differentiates the population also in terms of their future plans. Quite naturally, those who are in the high end see a faculty position for themselves at a four-year college or university as attractive. This is an overwhelming percentage in comparison to those who are less oriented to the university. However, the high group is also significantly higher on their seeing as very attractive a faculty position at another community or junior college or a position in a professional association. Those in the low group tend to view any faculty position or position in a professional association as unattractive. The people in the high group belong to more professional associations and attend meetings and present papers.

There is little relationship between one's reference group identification and how he views his students. The "university as reference group" construct did not distinguish between the way the people responded to the qualities that students should gain from a two-year college education. However, people in the high group tended to favor more humanities courses for students in occupational programs and to believe that there were too few extracurricular offerings in the humanities.

Many of the differences between people in the high and low ends of the "university as a reference group" construct may be perceived when this construct is correlated with the other constructs. There is a strong positive correlation between "university as reference group" and "preference for further preparation," "concern with the humanities," "functional potential," and "research orientation." Significant relationships with "satisfaction," "curriculum and instruction," and "concern for students" do not pertain.

Those faculty members who tend most to look to the university as their reference group form a modestly professionalized subgroup within the faculty. They are oriented to their teaching disciplines, to research, and to further professional preparation. They tend to be well integrated personalities. They are not particularly satisfied or dissatisfied, nor are they different in the way they view their students or their teaching. They are younger (some are graduate students working part-time) and have worked at their institution for a shorter time. They come from homes where there were many books, and they tend to read more scholarly journals within their field.

The people who look least to the university are the old-timers. They may well be chairpersons who have worked in their current institution for many years. They are less interested in further professional development and tend more toward nonprofessional activities in their free time.

The secondary school has nearly disappeared as a reference point. Although more than half the faculty have taught in secondary schools, only 11 percent of the entire group saw high school teachers as very useful sources of advice on teaching, ranking them barely ahead of college administrators. Some commentators have asserted that two-year college instructors would be better put to articulate their courses and methods with the local secondary schools than with the senior institutions. But this appears unlikely—the community college faculty have escaped from the secondary school and have no intention of looking back.

CHAPTER

13

THE ENDANGERED HUMANITIES

The humanities are for everyone. No matter where the person is, what his field of work or interests, he confronts some aspects of the humanities somewhere along the line. Even Socrates' early and pervasive adage to "know thyself" is rooted in humanistic thought. And whether one judges contemporary events on the basis of the past, or whether one is exposed to literary criticism or artistic appraisal, the humanities are involved.

Because the humanities pose alternative ways of thinking, allowing one to experience vicariously what otherwise might not be felt, they open the individual to an awareness of varying approaches. This awareness in turn becomes tantamount to stimulating flexibility. Thus, we firmly believe that exposure to the humanities acts as a counterforce to rigidity—not a trivial effect when we see what horror has been wrought by authoritarianism. We can draw pictures of very rigid people or we can look at slightly less extreme cases and perceive the difficulties encountered because movement of personality is constricted. Fairly recent examples of such restrictions occurred when the aircraft industry cut back severely, leaving vast numbers of engineers and other highly specialized workers jobless. Many of these people had the intelligence but not the inner flexibility to adjust to the new conditions fostered by economic shifts. It is difficult, at best, to assign causal relationships; but it would appear that those who had previously experienced alternatives—either vicariously or actually—were better able to make the transition than those who had not confronted such choices.

Outside of fostering flexibility, the humanities can provide pleasure in numerous ways. Whether one's choice is pop or rock, country or classic, music is one of the pleasures of life; music appreciation is a humanity. Whether one looks to Shakespeare or Faulkner, Fitzgerald or Bellow—the humanities are involved. Other illustrations apply to all the humanities—the delight in discovering cross-cultural similarities, the understanding of contemporary events in light of the past, and the opportunity to revel in sheer fantasy.

How, then, do people who teach the humanities perceive this broad area? What differences between humanities and other instructors pertain to the way they view the humanities? What are the differences among people who are more or less concerned with them? To answer these and related questions, a construct, "concern with humanities," was erected. This construct concentrates on specific attitudes and feelings regarding the humanities, its items including some that assess direct experiences with the humanities, others that pertain to teaching them.

Although we are concerned primarily with the humanities population as a whole, it is interesting to look at involvement in the humanities in terms of teaching disciplines. Here we note that considerably more people teaching history, literature, political science, and social science tend to be in the high "concern with humanities" group. Conversely, the low group includes more foreign language instructors.

Those instructors who had been students in community/junior colleges also tend toward the low "concern with humanities" group. More humanities instructors who are in the high group are working on their doctorates. When it comes to nonhumanities faculty, however, more of those working on the advanced degree tend to fall into the low "concern with humanities" group. There is a slight tendency for a greater percentage of males to fall into the high "concern with humanities" group. There is also a slight tendency for younger instructors to be in the high group.

Neither the fact that one has been an instructor or administrator in a secondary school or a four-year college or university nor the number of years one has been a faculty member has any consistent bearing on one's "concern with humanities." A slight tendency toward greater concern is found among department or division chairpersons. Chairpersonship and employment practices regarding doctorate holders similarly relate to humanities concern; a greater number of those who fall into the *low* "concern for humanities" group had previously hired people with the doctorate.

More humanities instructors who are in the high "concern with humanities" group tend to be full-time instructors than those who are in the low group. These people teach more than 10 to 12 hours per week and tend not to be employed at an additional job. If they are so employed, however, this is for 21 hours or more per week.

Of the eight sources of advice on teaching offered in the Faculty Survey, people highly concerned with the humanities tend to rate university professors higher than do the total sample. Other differences are minimal. As for journals, more in the low group neither subscribe to nor read journals.

Eighty-six percent of all respondents report they would like to take steps toward professional development in the next five years. People who are high in "concern with humanities," however, far outnumber those in the low group on this variable. While more low than high respondents would enroll in courses in a university, the reverse is true for earning the Ph.D. or Ed.D. degrees. More people in the high "concern with humanities" group tended to be members of professional organizations, attended regional or national meetings, and presented papers. If they had it to do over, they would study more humanities. On their own they tend to experience the humanities by visiting museums, shows, exhibits, concerts, theater, or films; reading; and listening to records, television, or radio. Interestingly, people low in "concern with humanities" are more inclined to feel that humanities courses had been added or improved at their colleges. More people in the high group would like to see the integration of humanities into interdisciplinary courses as well as more extracurricular courses.

People with a high concern with humanities tend to be well-integrated instructors, concerned also with curriculum and instruction and with their students. There is a strong negative correlation between "concern with humanities" and "satisfaction," however, suggesting that those most concerned with the humanities find an unsatisfactory climate for their efforts in the two-year college.

Interestingly, the respondents who taught in other than humanities fields seem to be little different from the humanities faculty on the construct "concern with humanities." It may be that chairpersons from other disciplines hold as firm a commitment to the overall aspects of two-year college education as do those within the humanities fields; hence, they see the virtue of some exposure to the humanities for their students. Whatever the case, the fact that they do see a place for the humanities suggests a wider range of involvement in humanities instruction than could be garnered if the humanities faculty relied only on students enrolling in their own courses and programs.

In association with the survey, we also gained information from people gathered at various meetings to discuss the findings. The idea of the humanities in two-year colleges was considered by administrators, division chairpersons, faculty members, and foundation officials at several conferences. Although many seemed to feel that humanities education at their colleges was declining, some claimed that it was very much a part of the total curriculum. At some colleges, at least one humanities course is required for any degree, including occupational and vocational programs; at others a core of humanities courses is required. The groups discussing the study suggested that there has been an increase in integrated humanities courses that incorporate interdisciplinary studies and employ teaching teams. Nonetheless, the groups seem to feel that the colleges on the whole tend not to be committed to education in the humanities. Many of the participants pointed out that humanities courses frequently are offered only to fulfill university-mandated transfer requirements or degree requirements imposed by accrediting agencies.

Relatively few students beginning college are concentrating in humanities programs. Instead, for fear of not finding employment, they are attracted to the career-oriented curriculums. If the humanities faculty were to attend only to students majoring in their disciplines, they would find few takers for their offerings. More students would be found in humanities courses required for those who would transfer to universities while majoring in other programs. Even more students could be affected if the humanities were integrated into the technical courses. The goal of humanities education is to train people, not technicians; hence the inclusion of humanistic elements in occupational courses is a distinct possibility. Humanities education need not be confined within traditional definitions nor implemented solely through traditional curriculum and instruction channels.

This note on the humanities is important because it suggests patterns of faculty involvement that run beyond the ordinary. Most instructors tend still to be concerned with students in their own field. They prefer offering credit courses that parallel those offered at senior institutions. It is easier for them to teach courses as they were taught, more difficult to explore new avenues for pursuing humanistic studies. The full-time instructors are indeed concerned with their students and with their teaching, but curriculum integration and the preparation of the modules in the humanities to be inserted in occupational courses, the creation of noncredit courses, and the delivery of humanities through other than course formats seem foreign to their thinking.

The faculty seem unaware of several overarching problems that affect enrollment in their programs and courses, and they seem unconcerned that the expansion in two-year college education occurs outside their own disciplines. By 1974 there were more part-time faculty than full-timers; and although 20 percent of the full-time faculty teach humanities, a constant figure over the years, only 10.7 percent of the part-timers do. The expansion in new college programs, hence in faculty employment, is in other areas—business and management, public affairs and services, home economics, cooperative work experience education, and computer and information sciences.

The interesting point is that many humanities instructors seem little concerned. As the full-time faculty shrinks, who will speak for the humanities? The part-timers have no power. The administrators have more things to consider than the diminution of traditional programs. The regular faculty seem to exhibit more concern for their own welfare than for their academic field. Their professional associations argue for higher wages and shorter hours. Their disciplinary associations may address the humanities; but when they do, they consider arcane teaching techniques and disciplinary esoterica. The faculty deplore their institutions' reducing course requirements and pandering to student desires for courses of immediate utility, but they take little aggressive action to stem these tides.

The instructor within the humanities is faced with a challenge. To maintain his position he need do nothing—work rules, faculty welfare practices, and tradition protect his own job. But his teaching field is not similarly protected. Subject to the vagaries of student interest and university transfer requirements, emphasis shifts from one program area to another. The expansion in course offerings takes place elsewhere. Yet, for most instructors, as long as they are protected in their own work this insidious assault on their teaching areas seems of little moment.

Individual instructors can respond by taking several steps. They can try to stay current in their discipline—the survey found that 23 percent of the full-time humanities instructors read no scholarly or professional journals. They can support their professional and disciplinary associations—fewer than half the full-timers had attended an association meeting in the three years prior to the survey; 90 percent of them had never presented a paper; 17 percent were not even nominal members. He can demand that his associations consider arcana less, issues of public policy more. In brief, he can break out of his insularity, his reclusivity, his concern only for a diminishing group of students taking an ever smaller number of humanities courses.

The instructor may well broaden his vision beyond his own institution. He can serve on program articulation committees and beseech the universities in his area to reinstitute language, history, and other humanities course requirements so students who intend transferring are obliged to take the courses. Yet, as laudable as this practice is, it is shortsighted—the direction of community college expansion is not toward augmenting enrollment of baccalaureate-bound students. It is toward the short course of immediate interest or utility for other types of clients. Further, the transfer students frequently circumvent the requirements by leaving the two-year college short of the associate degree; and the universities are glad to take them anyway.

The instructor who would expand his role could do more. Many instructors have gone into public programming, building objectives and criterion tests around major public broadcasts. Others have stepped outside their classroom and built reproducible learning packages that can be used by students without the instructor's intervention. Other full-time faculty members have tried to weave together the part-timers in their area, training them in writing objectives, sharing teaching strategies with them, and molding them into a faculty group worthy of the name, as contrasted with a group of individuals nominally concerned with teaching single courses. And still other instructors have vigorously promoted concerts, recitals, exhibits, and other noncourse-related programs at their own institutions.

The disciplinary associations in all academic fields tend too much to quibble over definitions and the esoteric aspects of their subject areas. Similarly, the professional associations are faculty welfare organizations. The individual instructor should address the main issues of support for the programs in which he believes. Federal, state, and local level funding runs not necessarily to programs where student learning in any form is maximized; its routings are determined by political processes. The instructor who has a commitment to his teaching field cannot hide behind his classroom door and await students who would attend to his ministrations. He must change his work orientation in the direction of a broader effort. The sciences, humanities, and arts must now be pursued through integrated courses, noncredit courses, public programs, and extracurricular activities. Astute and broad-minded faculty members realize this and work in these areas.

Taking a positive approach, the humanities should be seen as something other than archaic. They are not the property of fusty academics but are essential in the continuing debate over the quality of life. Certainly, the faculty should continue to train students who would become specialists but, in the community college, these are a small and shrinking minority. The humanities can well be broadened beyond the classroom as a way of bringing them to public attention. Not only students but all members of the public can be encouraged to raise questions about the kind of genetic modifications we should have, the quality of air and water, the patterns of energy use, the kind of life that should be led. This type of thinking about the uses of the discipline leads an instructor to understand that his influence can be made much more far reaching than if he remains in his classroom teaching only those who happen to come in.

CHAPTER
14
THE FUTURE OF
THE COLLEGE

This book has recounted information obtained from a major national survey of two-year college faculty members. As such it presents a picture of people in a professional group functioning in an academic institution. We have not attempted to compare these instructors with their counterparts at other levels or types of institutions because we feel the two-year colleges are large enough and important enough to stand on their own as an area of interest. The nearly 200,000 people who work within them should be considered as a unit worthy of analysis in its own right.

We have seen the faculty as an occupational group that has not yet developed its own professional image. Two-year college instructors are anxious to be identified with higher or postsecondary education, concerned that they not be considered as secondary school instructors. Yet their own image has not emerged. Instead, they seem to combine elements emanating from both secondary schools and the senior institutions but not sufficiently clear to be defined uniquely.

In considering the future of the faculty it is necessary to look carefully at the institution in which they work. The university began as a housing for researchers; the four-year college as an academy training people for the learned professions; the secondary school as an agency of enculturation. Each has undergone its own metamorphosis and taken on a form quite different from that which it presented when it began.

What of the two-year college? Here also is change in form and image over the years. Beginning as a lower division school offering the first two years of traditional college-level studies or as a postsecondary finishing school, the college later added occupational and adult education, guidance activities, and community services. Its patterns reflect the broadening of higher education in the twentieth century. It matriculates students across the entire age range of the population; it allows all to enter regardless of previous academic success; and it offers certificate programs that ever increasingly compress the liberal arts.

It is not difficult to speculate on the future of the two-year colleges. Events move slowly in educational institutions, and colleges in the next decade or two will not be much different from those of today. Many of the people who now work in the colleges will still be there at the turn of the century, maintaining their current conception of what constitutes a proper college education, lining up then as they do now on the side of more or less emphasis on occupational training, more or less liberal or general education. The colleges need not be assessed in light of a brave new world but only as they accommodate to existing forms of governance, funding, and curriculum instruction.

The number of colleges will change, although not as markedly as in recent decades. The pattern of institutional development points toward their expanding until each state includes a college within reasonable daily commuting distance of nearly every resident. When a state reaches this saturated stage, new colleges are opened only when shifts in the population occur. Several have already reached this level of maturity: Washington, Florida, California, Michigan, Illinois, Ohio, and New York. If the number of colleges in all states expands to a comparable relationship with area and population, the nation will top out at approximately 1,400 institutions, or about 200 more than were in operation in 1976. (This leveling of growth is predicated on the assumption that a sizable proportion of the private junior colleges will merge or close. These institutions have displayed no growth since the 1950s, and many of them will be forced to go public or to effect liaisons with senior institutions.)

If the definition of "community college" is modified to include a variety of adult schools, technical institutes, and occupational training centers not now covered within its scope, the numbers could change drastically. There is some indication that this is happening—witness the recent changes in the title of the directory published by the American Association of Community and Junior Colleges: from *Junior College Directory* (pre-1972), to *Community and Junior College Directory* (1973-74), to *Community, Junior, and Technical College Directory* (1975). If even more institutional types are brought in under the rubric, the projected figure of 1,400 might easily be doubled. South Carolina and Wisconsin, for example, have entire systems of technical colleges organized apart from their two-year university branches. Both types of institutions are usually counted as "two-year colleges." But Pennsylvania's two-year university branches, formerly in the *Directory*, were dropped. Definitional modification is more influential on changes in numbers of colleges than is typical expansion.

All colleges in all states will not take the same form. There are now—there have always been—differences in curriculum emphasis. Where opportunities for postsecondary education in four-year colleges are high—such as in Connecticut, Pennsylvania, Ohio, and Massachusetts—the two-year colleges may well accommodate themselves to a curriculum of occupational offerings along with remedial studies and college-parallel courses for students who either are not admissible to the senior institutions or who choose to stay at home and go to the local college.

Organizational forms will not change much. The colleges now fall into four main organizational types: private, independent, or church-related; two-year branch campuses of senior institutions; colleges founded by local school districts and supported with some assistance from the state; and state-level managed colleges. The pattern of organization in coming years will follow these lines, with emphasis on the institutions governed at the local level and supported with state funds, Although funds will be distributed more equitably among districts in each state, a corresponding trend toward state-level control of curriculum will not perforce develop. Colleges offering programs that reflect the tendencies of the residents of their district will remain the dominant type. The current trend toward localism and the acceptance of diversity and plurality in populations could sustain a network of colleges funded in common pattern, but each with its own particular characteristics. However, without vigorous effort by local leaders to maintain their colleges' distinctiveness and responsiveness, the tendency toward imitation that propels institutions toward commonality will take hold. Here they will recreate the history of the secondary schools, becoming distressingly similar certifying agencies and custodial institutions.

In states where a community college has been built within commuting distance of practically every person, many educators have sought to maintain growth by establishing the two-year colleges as the institution where all students would begin their postsecondary education. Indeed, by the mid-1970s, 90 percent of those who began college in California began in a two-year institution. However, that state had the most mature system of publicly accessible postsecondary education; and, although the concept seemed destined to spread into most other states, it has been stymied. One problem is that the traditional 18- to 21-year-old college age group stopped expanding in number and seems destined to remain stabilized well into the 1990s. This means that the universities and four-year institutions are faced with declining enrollments if they abandon their lower division students to the two-year colleges, something that few seem willing to do. Instead they began competing by offering their own subbaccalaureate programs.

Another limitation on two-year colleges expanding along traditional lines is that many of their spokesmen see their institution's role as providing other than lower-division education for everyone in the community. This has led to the rise of noncampus-based structures—courses in church basements and store fronts all over the district—and noncredit programs. Whether these programs are offered under the stamp of recertification, community service, or any other, they are clearly different from the degree-credit courses typical of a lower division institution. The colleges may grow, but in a different direction.

Institutional management also is changing. In the future, local governing boards will still operate much as they do now, but management will be a process of accommodation among contending forces. The last vestiges of paternalism will soon disappear under the press of employee bargaining units. The corps of functionaries and bureaucrats that has already taken its place alongside the professional educators will grow because state and federal level demands for data and information used in cost accounting will become ever greater. The college will not be managed by amateurs—the lower schools evidence the difficulties of an institution's reverting to the citizenry once it has come under the management of professionals. Hence, "community control" will make few inroads.

College control and management are important to, but far removed from, the instructors' daily life. Their students and the curriculum they teach have far greater influences on the role they adopt and on their feelings about their work. Students force role shifts in many ways. Interested, bright, dedicated, self-motivated students evoke different instructor role orientations from those yielded in response to dull, lethargic, hostile, and disinterested clients. Students affect curriculum too. If they are disinclined to study in a certain field, no amount of fiscal intervention in equipment and laboratories, no measure of cajolery by counselors and instructors will change their thinking. In recent years foreign language enrollments have dropped; personal interest course enrollments have expanded. If students prefer backpacking, scuba diving, and trim 'n slim, no number of throw-out-the-ball physical education instructors can persuade them to participate in team sports.

Further, the very idea of curriculum is shifting. Even now a community college curriculum cannot accurately be viewed in classical terms; it is not a coherent integrated sequence of courses and experiences. In fact, regardless of how the programs are designed, they are not sequential at all for most of the students who enroll in them. A sizable majority of students do not complete planned programs—vocational, transfer, academic major, or anything else. They drop in and out, changing majors, beginning programs without completing them, using the institution as an ever present resource. For them, the college is a reflexive, passive institution. Traditional concepts of curriculum view it as time-based with programs spanning months or years. But although community college catalogs still address curriculum in those terms, the students have effectually modified it.

If the two-year college curriculum is to be seen in terms other than classical curriculum theory, what conceptualizations might be made? Taking as a point of departure the experiences that the student undergoes, the college and its curriculum can be seen as a series of spectator events, an accessible place for social interaction, an institution that offers credentials, or an area where one learns to manipulate tools and concepts to try out his ideas. Each of these conceptualizations leads to a different view of the institution and to the people who work within it.

There is much precedent for the college as a series of spectator events. Most colleges now display deliberate spectacles such as planetarium exhibits, art shows, theater performances, and concerts. Students and members of the broader community can benefit from these types of events even as they can from patterned courses. Instructors can organize these events just as they organize traditional programs, but a different work orientation is required.

The college as a place of social interaction is similarly well known. Here is where those who had predicted that learning would take place over a television console in the home, who felt that reproducible broadcast media obviated the necessity for bringing students to schoolhouses, were proved wrong. The social aspects of the school, well known to those educational philosophers who have long felt that the most important benefits to be derived from the institution accrued thereby, became dominant. People tend to create their own entertainment, learning from each other in social environments. People interacting together satisfy each other's demands in ways that cannot be accommodated when they sit alone in their own homes. It becomes increasingly difficult for an instructor to justify remaining aloof, meeting classes, and then leaving campus.

The college as a dispenser of certificates allowing people to move into better paying or more satisfying jobs is similarly familiar. Call it training, retraining, upgrading skills, or whatever—when an employer demands credentials, the two-year college will respond by providing them. Credit for experience, credit by examination, short courses leading to various degrees and certificates— all are built on a realization that the college must provide what people need. As long as the United States is a society that recognizes credentials, this curriculum form will be a part of two-year college education. Instructors either build the criteria for the credentials or surrender their authority.

All these purposes must not be ignored in a conceptualization of the two-year college curriculum and the faculty role therein. The idea of the college as enhancing its students' awareness, skills, and ability to handle tools and concepts must be tempered with considerations of these variant purposes. They also conflict with the idea of a rational scientific procedure for curriculum development. Those who hold to this notion recommend taking all individual and social needs and putting them into a comprehensive plan along with individual learning styles, forecasts of future job markets and living patterns, and changing cultural contexts. The fond dream of community college advocates is that the institution be instantly responsive to all these concepts and the interactions among them. But this is not to be. Legislators look at student flow-through data and credits earned as a ratio of dollars expended. Local taxpayers may be satisfied with the colleges' spectator events. The administrators grope to manage what little discretion is left to them after the local and state governing boards have built in ever more rules. The faculty turns to its bargaining agents, whose primary concern is the welfare of the membership. Curriculum development is not, has not been, and is not likely to become a rational, predictable process. It takes place in a political arena within the colleges as individual instructors, program heads, and departments vie for support. It takes place extramurally as lobby groups, employers, and social action agencies contend for programs that address their own concerns.

Curriculum shifts are impossible to preduct accurately, but some changes seem imminent. To avoid slipping out from under the tent of higher education that they so laboriously entered around the middle of the century, the community colleges will become more rigorous in defining the distinctions between courses for credit and presentations or events open to the public. They will retain their preeminence in adult basic education and college-parallel courses, adding high level technical programs to their occupational offerings. Programs for periodic recertification of semiprofessional personnel will expand markedly. But infinite expansion into occupational training that is properly the responsibility of unions and industrial enterprises will cease. Much of the lower-order occupational training, such as the construction trades and food services, will revert to apprenticeships sanctioned by the unions but for which college credits are offered.

This is not to say that the curriculum will become more homogeneous and well defined. Even now the distinctions among curriculum patterns are not clear. What passes for "community services" in one institution is "adult education" in another; and "occupational" program in one college is "college parallel" in yet another, if the senior institution in its area will accept courses in the program for undergraduate credit. The most distinctive trend in curriculum now is that the holistic graded sequence that presumes to provide its graduates with a distinctive garb is becoming progressively weaker, falling under the onslaught of mass higher education. In its place are short courses for personal interest and modular programs that train for specific tasks. The graded curriculum will not die easily—certification requirements will bolster it in technical and professional programs—but it will be severely diminished.

As curriculum develops in coming years, the faculty and administrators will be forced to realize that its main distinctions are not between "academic" and "occupational" programs—a spurious dichotomy—but between "courses" and "presentations." Conceptually a course must include specific instructional objectives and an assessment of student learning. That is why students should be able to obtain course credit for learning realized elsewhere. A "presentation" or series of events may have all the apparent elements of a course—scheduled time, calendar, lecture, media—but, typically, it does not include defined objectives or learning outcomes. As educators and legislators become aware of the differences between the two, the practice of awarding course credit for attending presentations will subside.

College-parallel programs may well reform around ad hoc, short, flexible current-interest courses. Today, for example, where the humanities are strong they are centered on courses in film appreciation rather than the study of literature; the social sciences on consumerism rather than on traditional disciplinary studies. This is, in fact, the beginning of a merger of the liberal arts with leisure-time pursuits, a reversion to the origins of liberal arts. The liberal arts will be studied for their own sake with students enrolling in courses that fit their own interests in literature, cinema, and art.

A form of college not yet seen will develop around the idea of community services. Many colleges now have more hobby courses and adult enrichment activities than either traditional college programs or occupational training sequences. We may soon see a split with entire institutions created and maintained solely to provide these types of activities for people in their district. Call it adult education, life-long learning, education for leisure time pursuits, or any other appelation, here is where postsecondary education will demonstrate a reversion to one of its original purposes: the pursuit of knowledge for the sake of the pleasure it provides.

Nonetheless, there are problems associated with building the nonlinear curriculum onto the college form. Funding patterns in two-year colleges have traditionally been tied to average daily attendance or to the number of students completing a graded curriculum. Faculty salaries, evaluation procedures, and self-definition have been tied to courses. Community perceptions of college as a campus-based form also intrude and assign a peripheral status to other than "college level" programs. The greatest problem faced by the community colleges in the last quarter of the twentieth century is the modification of these fixed systems, procedures, and perceptions in response to their desire to broaden their offerings.

The community colleges in coming years will not be concerned as much with ways to award credit for learning attained elsewhere, but with the resolution of jurisdictional disputes between themselves and both the public schools' adult education divisions and university extension centers that, even now, offer similar curriculums. A view of the community as a whole as the proper target of college concern would allow the community colleges to transcend both the secondary schools and the universities from which they sprang. But this will not come about soon because of the intensely modified perceptions of education that it requires and because of the competitive nature of institutions.

In coming years, community colleges will repeatedly effect liaisons with the proprietary schools that offer various types of occupational and technical training. Occupational training centers will continue to provide many educational services, but students will receive credit from the community colleges. A precedent for this type of cooperative relationship between institutions can be found as long ago as the nineteenth century, when the universities widened their umbrella to include art and architectural ateliers and scientific institutes, which eventually became part of the broader university itself.

Curriculum will be varied between states and, in many cases, within states. Community college curriculums may be based on the traditional comprehensive model, which sees the same institution offering occupational programs along with college-parallel courses. However a growing number of colleges even now offer occupational training almost exclusively, with the humanities and social and natural sciences diminished almost to the point of extinction. This split will be accentuated, and for some states the postsecondary occupational training center will serve as the model for their community colleges. Cooperative training with industrial establishments will be a feature of these institutions.

These variations in curricular emphases will not invariably follow particular organizational or governance patterns. Although the private colleges, for example, typically sustain liberal arts and college-parallel curriculums, many of them offer current interest courses of a type that would qualify as community service in the public institutions. In keeping with their traditions, many of them may turn to providing the finishing school type of educational services that the public colleges cannot well offer because of their nonresidential character.

In coming years the tendency toward awarding credit for experience will subside because the colleges will not surrender their trump card—the degree—without adequate remuneration. However, the United States is and will remain a credential society; thus, an institution that sanctions learning wherever achieved will be needed. Other agencies will certainly arise to certify people for learning attained through self-study. Although the value of the associate degree will have been severely deflated—even as the high school diploma is deflated today—there will still be need for job certification.

Where is the faculty in all this? Much depends on the patterns of professionalization that develop, but one thing is certain—the model of a college governed by its faculty members will soon disappear. The nonacademic manager will become an even more prominent figure in institutional life than he is at present. Probably but not as certainly, instructors' roles will tend toward specialization. People will do different types of teaching tasks, less housekeeping. The specializations will include people who will operate through reproducible media only, those who serve as tutors spread throughout the community, those who act as managers of a corps of aides. As the competition from other media becomes ever stronger even as the ability of the institution to command student attendance as a rite of passage becomes weaker, teaching will be seen as a combination of instruction and entertainment. Thus a teacher might adopt any of several roles: the full-time faculty member performing all tasks within an institution that is managed by nonacademic personnel (the high school model); the full-time highly paid program head or laboratory manager working with a corps of hourly rate instructors and laboratory technicians; the 40-hour-a-week teacher in a graded occupational curriculum; or the part-time instructor of continuing education and/or entertainment courses that ebb and flow in accordance with demand. Other roles are suggested in the following chapter.

CHAPTER

15

THE FUTURE OF
THE FACULTY

The Faculty Survey and other recent observations have led us to speculate on the future of the faculty. What will they become, collectively and individually? How will they see their role and responsibilities? In what directions will unionization and institutional modification of mission propel them?

Historically, the role of the faculty has been to meet classes, develop curriculum, advise and interact with students, prepare instructional media, maintain the scholarly standards of an academic institution, and attend to certain aspects of institutional management. But as the colleges and their curriculum have shifted, so have the faculty. They have magnified some features of their working life, reduced others, and denied some totally. As of now, few instructors accept instruction as a discipline, even as most have lost contact with their parent academic discipline. Few are concerned with management; most have refused to become involved with the moving ideas of the community college. Few are concerned with long range curricular or instructional planning; most hide behind their classroom doors and wait for decisions made by others. These instructors are not only those best characterized as the time-servers or clock punchers who seek only to reduce their working hours. They include also the instructors who genuinely feel they are involved in their teaching because they meet students daily but who are, in fact, not developing within the profession, not using the profession to enhance their own growth as human beings, not advancing the profession itself.

We would pose a new way of characterizing these instructors. We see them as recluses, isolated from the academic disciplines in which they were trained, from the universities and the secondary schools, and from the broad currents of the two-year colleges, their host institutions. They are in an eddy away from the mainstream, and they have placed themselves there of their own volition.

This is not to say that all faculty other than those who are advancing the profession are reclusive. Nor is it to say that those who are, are perforce cut off from other aspects of their life; they may be quite related to family, friends, students, and like-minded colleagues. But it is worth exploring the faculty member as a recluse as an aid in understanding the way many instructors behave in relation to their work.

The reclusive complex stems from three phenomena, one relating to the teacher as a human being and academician, another to recent developments in the community college field, the third with teaching itself.

HUMAN ATTITUDES OF TEACHERS

A teacher's attitudes toward teaching are undoubtedly shaped by his own personality, early experiences, mentors, colleagues, the institutional climate—a complex of prior and coterminous events. The role itself plays a part. As long ago as 1932 Willard Waller traced this effect. In *The Sociology of Teaching* he discussed the phenomenon of teaching as one of conflict, with the individual on one occasion saying to the student, "I am your teacher. Do as I say!" and on the other, "But I am also a human being and a good fellow. We have some good times together, don't we?" He identified this rhythmic contraction and expansion of the instructor's personality as having an insidious effect on the person.

Others have also noted the problem of reconciling two personalities: the human being and the instructor. In her intensive study of a group of two-year college faculty members, Leslie Purdy discussed how a person may have some basic orientation toward teaching, may have a picture of self in role, "but once on the job, the attitudes are altered and shaped by peer attitudes and norms, by experiences from teaching itself, and by other aspects of the teaching environment." This is a private environment, one with jealously guarded covenants regarding work space. Purdy discerned that

> One attitude toward teaching expressed by many teachers . . . is that teaching is and should be a solo activity, one teacher and one or more students. The privateness and the self-sufficiency of teachers in a classroom is a cherished part of teaching. Many instructors resisted any teaching method which would require sharing responsibility with another person for a class. . . . Deciding what will go on in a course and then enacting that plan is seen as a personal challenge to each teacher. . . . A common understanding existed that each teacher privately and individually face his or her own teaching. No one can stand in for another teacher . . . (1973, p. 177).

Most teachers, Purdy points out, feel a need for hands-on involvement to get feedback from their students. This leads them to be possessive about their classes. Many instructors translate the idea of academic freedom as "my right to do what I want in my class." Further, Purdy related how

> Instructors would only accept advice from someone else who had gone through the fires, experienced the traumas and successes of teaching. Recommendations about a new teaching method coming from faculty members are more likely to be considered by teachers while information presented by administrators . . . can be ignored. (1973, p. 181).

These attitudes are not confined to the two-year college level. David Riesman has noted how faculty

> are oriented . . . to students and teaching and are often inimical to discipline and to disciplines and to what they see as dehydrated specialization. Sometimes they use unionization and sometimes evaluation by students to protect themselves from the need for scholarly visibility both inside and outside their institutions. Academia is witnessing a new provincialism—not the provincialism of one's discipline, . . . but the perhaps more destructive or insidious, although less evident, provincialism of captivity by one's student disciples, charismatically courted as the road not only to retention but to feelings of worth (1976, p. 12).

What is happening is that a new ethos is taking hold, one in which faculty take pride in severing themselves from outside ideas as well as from outside people. And if Riesman has seen this phenomenon in the university, where there has been a tradition of scholarship and cosmopolitanism, think how much more it is accentuated in the two-year college, whose roots are in the local community, where academic disciplinary affiliation has always been weak. The Faculty Survey found 26 percent of the respondents who, by their own admission, read *no* scholarly journals; 64 percent who read *no* journals related to professional education or to teaching in their field. More than 90 percent said their colleagues were, "quite useful" or "somewhat useful" as sources of advice on teaching, and nearly the same number found students, "quite useful" or "somewhat useful." Department chairpersons, university professors, professional journals, programs of professional organizations, high school teachers, and administrators were far down on the line as other choices, in that order. Also, the faculty teaching in the humanities—history, literature, philosophy, and so on— were found to be little more committed to the humanities than were the comparison group of instructors in other areas. The lines of an *a*disciplinary group emerged, one that had abandoned the academic and not replaced it with anything of substance.

CHANGING ROLES OF TWO-YEAR COLLEGE TEACHERS

The pattern of college development has much to do with the instructor's shrinking away from outside ideas. Consider the teacher of academic courses who began his career in the 1950s or 1960s. When he came into the institution it was billed as the first two years of college. His courses were to be equivalent to those offered at a four-year college or university. Certainly there were vocational programs, but they were offered in another building somewhere else, on a different part of the campus. Certainly there was the problem of accommodating students of low ability; but there were not many of them, and one could always fail them without excessive concern.

By the 1970s, the institutions seemed to have gone into some other business. The occupational programs grew ever larger. There seemed to be more low ability students, more remedial courses. And what was this "community-based education" that the instructor heard so much about? He might have accepted the move toward remedial work—at least it took the form of courses with students sitting in the classroom; there was some relationship to academic teaching. But one-day programs on purchasing real estate? Giving credit to people who used the college's swimming pool on hot summer days? The instructor might be forgiven for thinking that the college was saying, in effect, "We have given up trying to remedy student defects in reading, ability to analyze arguments, values, and logical interpretation—the traditional role of general education—and we are going to pander to community desires for entertainment and recreation." What was left for the instructor? Whatever affinity he once had for history, literature, biology, or philosophy was eroded by his lack of affiliation with like-minded members of those disciplines over the years. He could reduce content to satisfy remedial students and still have a course retain some semblance of itself. But what was he to make of the funds and recognition that were going into health fairs, community art projects, and modular courses on "How to Deal in the Commodities Market"?

In the 1950s and 1960s, when most faculty were recruited from secondary schools, there was a feeling of challenge in the new level of education. The move from high school to college brought a perceived increase in status along with a reduction in the number of required teaching hours from 30 to 15. Greater status and half a teaching load—quite a giant step! The high growth rate in the 1950s and 1960s also meant that, for the individual instructor, there were new colleagues to be indoctrinated and the excitement that goes with establishing new relationships.

But by the 1970s there was no place to move. The period of high growth had ended. The instructor in the two-year college could not realistically aspire to a position in a four-year institution—even though three-fourths of the respondents to the Faculty Survey said they would find a position in a four-year college or university "attractive." That door was open to very few. The senior institutions had many sources of instructors and they tended not to look to people who had been socialized at another level of education.

There were other changes. In many colleges part-timers who were paid on an hourly rate were being used to fill classes whenever a full-timer retired or left the institution for any reason. Frequently employed at the last minute, the part-timers had little affinity for the institution, and certainly little if any contact with the full-time instructors. What was the full-time instructor to make of this tendency? Data from the Faculty Survey revealed that part-time instructors differ from full-timers in that the part-timers are less experienced and read fewer scholarly or professional journals; are less likely to be members of professional associations, concerned with research, with curriculum and instruction, or with the humanities; and more likely to hold the university as a reference group. Clearly this was a different type of population, one with which the full-time instructor had little in common. Inexorably, year after year, the percentage of courses taught by this variant group grows larger. Might the full-timer be excused for wondering what happened to the ideal of consistency in curriculum, collegial interaction, and the commonality of instructional objectives or desired learning outcomes?

Yet, why should the part-time faculty not be growing in number? They meet their classes, give their lectures, hear student recitals, turn their grades in on time. Put another way, what can the full-time faculty do that the part-timers cannot? Certainly the full-timers have more experience, read more journals, are more concerned with curriculum and instruction, more interested in research. They are, but what do they *do*? What is that body of specialized knowledge that they bring to bear on problems of instruction? Are they more likely to employ specific measurable objectives or validated criterion-referenced testing devices? Are they more likely to report student learning in terms that have a clear and consistent referent? The answer is that as the full-timers insist on closing the door to their classroom and hiding behind perquisites in their contract, so no one knows the extent to which their students have learned, it is impossible to tell. Until evidence reveals that their students learn more than students taught by the part-timers, why should a district hire full-timers at all, with the necessity of paying them more salary and fringe benefits and being obligated to them for continuity of employment? Judicial decisions and legislation may soon change this; it will not change because of the full-time faculty's initiative.

Institutional size too has had an effect on the faculty. The Faculty Survey revealed some information about instructors' relatedness. On a projective question asking how respondents saw themselves in relation to different groups listed, the larger the college the higher the percentage of instructors who saw the administrators as a tightly knit group, with the instructor himself standing apart from it. Further, the larger the college, the higher the percentage of instructors who saw themselves as standing apart from their teacher colleagues. Clearly as the colleges grow larger—and by 1976 one-half the faculty in American two-year colleges were teaching in institutions with greater than 10,000 enrollment—the faculty sense of relatedness diminishes. This is yet another cause, and effect, of the reclusive complex. If the faculty had developed a sense of common goals, techniques, concerns—a unique ethos—they would have had something to fall back on. As it is, they have done little but stand aside.

INSTRUCTIONAL MODIFICATION

The conflict between person and academician and the changes in college size and mission both affected the instructor. There is yet a third set of phenomena having to do with teaching. The two-year college is a self-styled "teaching institution." However, the calls for innovation heard so frequently in the 1960s have diminished. Whether or not they yielded much depends on one's interpretation. Certainly teaching practices have been modified somewhat; and many faculties are well along with televised instruction, learning laboratories, the offering of self-paced learning opportunities, and other instructional modifications. But consider the obstacles. First, there are few criteria for concluding that the innovation enhances student learning to a greater degree than the technique it replaces. Few faculty members have defined the outcomes of their courses so clearly that they can assess the relative value of one technique or another. Second, many innovations were brought in by administrators who were convinced that they had the potential for saving money. But rather than following through cost savings that could be obtained through deliberate assessment of cost/outcome relationships, when the financial crunch came the administrators took the easy way and began replacing full-time instructors with hourly rate part-timers.

Still, the cut that affected the individual instructor most is that he tended not to be rewarded for his efforts at instructional modification. Undoubtedly, changing an instructional technique is hard work; and the true manager of student learning must put in more hours in instructional planning than does his counterpart who delivers ad hoc lectures and unvalidated quizzes. But he has little access to assistance. The colleges have only relatively small budgets for instructional aides, readers, or teaching assistants that can be assigned to individual faculty members. Further, the instructional innovator has low visibility in his own college, even less outside it. Should he choose to attempt to meet with like-minded instructors in other parts of the nation he finds poorly defined professional associations in the teaching of his subject field and few funds for travel to meetings. The faculty member who has pursued innovation in his own teaching has had to do so out of a sense of professional obligation and a dedication to the belief that he can help his students learn more if he modifies his technique from the lecture/discussion/recital mode. It is not surprising that relatively few instructors have taken these options.

More to the point, consider how the reclusive complex comes into play here. The instructor who would be the innovator in managing student learning is put in a curious position. As he changes his instructional techniques—builds reproducible instructional programs, a learning laboratory, test-item banks—he may well find himself the subject of scorn. Small wonder. His actions implicitly call his colleagues' techniques into question. If he is a proselytizer, he may be met with derision. If he chooses to go his own way, he has "sold out to the administration." Purdy notes,

> Few teachers will single-handedly adopt practices which move them too far from the norms and practices of colleagues. . . . The few teachers who do break with their divisions or subject-matter groups to aggressively pursue a new practice either find a new faculty reference group in another division or relate themselves very closely to administrators and support staff members.

That is why many instructional innovators have become program heads, laboratory managers, instructional coordinators—all titles that at once evidence budget lines through which assistance in the form of media technicians and other aides can be provided, while at the same time setting these instructors apart from the rank and file. The group is by no means a majority in any institution, but it grows steadily. And the others become ever more isolated. Not all the faculty see themselves as managers. Not all the faculty who see themselves as managers of student learning become program heads—and not all program heads so define themselves. But all managers of learning are set apart. Sometimes they move to another department. Sometimes they stay where they are, effecting liaison with administrators to gain needed assistance but covering it so their colleagues do not dissociate themselves.

The use of objectives, media, and valid tests has little to do with the subject matter taught—lecturers, discussion leaders, learning laboratory managers, and videotape producers can be found in every field. It has to do with the instructor's interpretation of self in role. The difference between a traditional full-time faculty member and a manager of student learning is in that interpretation. One says, "The ideal learning situation is a few students together with me in a classroom. I like that best. It is comfortable. Students *must* learn thereby. I need not submit evidence that they have." The manager, on the other hand, sees student learning as the prime requisite and defines his own worth only to the extent that his students *did* learn. He assesses learning not only to aid his teaching but also for his own sake. Yet, he recognizes that a student may learn with or without his intervention; hence, he is free to adopt or reject reproducible media as appropriate.

Here, then, is a group growing not rapidly but steadily. The program coordinators manage learning laboratories, instructional aides, and otherwise identify themselves with the discipline of instruction. And the full-time faculty stands aside, unable to retard them, uncertain of their own position. Too long they held to the pseudoacademic freedom of the closed classroom door. Too long they spent themselves in efforts to reduce class size. Too long they defined themselves as valuable to the extent they had personal contact with students, resisting any suggestion that they align themselves with defined learning. For certain, they are protected temporarily; but they must watch the growth in staffing that is taking place among the part-timers. They must watch their colleagues being replaced with others not of their ilk.

The full-time faculty members who isolate themselves in their classrooms—certainly, they believe, for all good intentions—are the recluses. They have chosen to seal themselves away from trends, both in ideas relating to community college education, and in power. In recent years the community college has tended toward community education, adult education, off-campus activities. Yet the faculty members who see their primary mission as a process of cloistering themselves in classrooms, teaching traditional academic subjects, are not part of this movement.

Similarly, the faculty has pulled itself away repeatedly—one is tempted to say suicidally—from the lines of power within and around the colleges. The faculty have never been in a position of being institutional managers responsible for setting policy; that power has always rested with the board and the administration. But we now see faculty members refusing even to serve on college committees where at least the illusion of power is still present. We see faculty refusing to become members of speakers bureaus, where they would interact with the community in their areas of presumed expertise. "Serve on a committee? Go off-campus to speak? Why should I?" This is the reclusive complex in full blush.

Until the faculty adopts a guiding ethos, until it emerges from its isolation, it is, and will continue to be, a relatively unprofessionalized group comprised of individuals who pride themselves on privacy, cut themselves away from academic affiliation, refuse to attempt to understand the discipline of instruction, ignore ideas stemming from outsiders, scorn administrators, shun the community, abandon the part-timers who teach the same courses, treat with derision its own members who have become managers of student learning. The faculty have become isolated within their own institutions.

Although most instructors have become reclusive, some have borne up and begun defining their professional life in other ways. To do so requires a sizable measure of individual sensitivity and expertise along with an intense desire to become one's own person in the face of an environment that itself may not enhance that type of development. In *Education as a Profession*, Myron Lieberman said, "The factor which basically determines whether an individual will conduct himself professionally is whether or not the occupation is organized to insure a high level of service regardless of the individual motivations for

entering the profession or for rendering professional services in specific situations" (1956, pp. 221–22). In short, the way in which an individual acts is not
so much dependent on his motivation as it is on the roles laid down by the profession and the degree to which the profession is willing and able to enforce
those rules.

FACULTY PROFESSIONALISM

Is there a coherent definition of professionalization that can be applied to
two-year college instructors? To what extent does the group measure up? How is
it likely to develop? In viewing the faculty as professionals, the determinants of
a profession should be recounted. A profession is different from a craft, a trade,
or an occupation. To qualify for the term, "professional," the members of an
occupational group should display an element of peer judgment or self-policing,
an authoritative performance on behalf of a client or audience, a body of specialized knowledge not readily available to laymen, an internal or communal
sense of identity, a long period of training, a formal organization, and a code of
ethics. In fact, a group's tendencies toward professionalization and proximity to
professionalism are measured by the extent to which it reveals these characteristics.

Within the two-year college the question of peer judgment has not been
resolved. In recent years, the faculty in many states have attempted to fight off
legislators and members of governing boards who wanted more direct influence
on decisions regarding employment, maintenance of tenure, and dismissal.
Despite the fact that faculty evaluation begins with peer review, ultimate power
remains with the district. The faculty have not developed guidelines for self-
policing. Rare is the faculty group that recommends that one of its members
should be disciplined. Judicial decisions on rules of procedure have more to do
with who remains a member of the profession or who is required to leave it than
does the profession itself. The trend is toward protectionism; and, as negotiated
contracts become more prevalent, protection, not judging the members, will
become even more a characteristic of the faculty.

The idea of an authoritative performance on behalf of a client or an
audience has also changed recently. As faculty members prepare reproducible
media, they remove themselves from personal interaction with their clients.
Those who stay in the classroom seem to be protecting their right to perform for
their clients. But as others make decisions about awarding credit for experience
and credit by examination, the faculty's authority is diminished. Authoritativeness can be won only by the profession's providing a service not elsewhere available. Whether the faculty can convince their clients that their work is pro-
foundly important or that it includes aesthetic qualities not elsewhere available
is still an open question.

To the extent the faculty adhere to their academic discipline or to the discipline of instruction, they display a body of specialized knowledge not readily available to laymen. Some, of course, are quite skillful in their teaching. Others merely go through the motions. The difficulty is in tracing the outlines of the requisite activities in teaching. The study of an academic field or a trade for the six years or so that it takes for a faculty member to become certified undoubtedly places that person in possession of a considerable degree of knowledge that is not readily available to those who have not studied it. But although this holds for the subject area itself, it is not as readily apparent in the discipline of instruction that lacks an infrastructure of research, advocacy, and dissemination. In short, teaching is still a craft, as was engineering before Newton and Galileo and medicine before Harvey and Lister. In the absence of organizing principles, each practitioner learns his own tricks and makes ad hoc adjustments. The act of teaching still lacks theoretical justification.

The professional element of a communal identity is tied to the perceptions held by the members. Here the faculty seem to fall short. They seem not highly concerned with their academic field. They tend not to be affiliated with disciplinary organizations or, if they are members, they tend not to go to the meetings. They read few scholarly journals. They interact with each other more on questions of rights, welfare, and college level concerns than on issues relating to their doing a better job for their clients. Much in the community college acts to reduce academic affiliations. In the smaller institutions people teach in two or three subject areas and lose contact with the field outside their college and with the university programs in which they were prepared. Yet even those people who teach in only one disciplinary area seem always to find something to do other than to read and remain current in their discipline. The language of instruction, which depends so much on clear definition of desired outcomes, is rarely heard. Whatever communal identity there is among faculty tends not to run along the liens of a higher quality of ministration to those in their keeping.

One of the elements of a profession is that it be so recognized by outsiders. This seems not the case with the faculty. The lay person can be forgiven for feeling that the members of an occupational group that fails to define, in terms with common referent, just what they are trying to do are somewhat less than fully professionalized. The observer may also wonder why the faculty cling so tenaciously to organizations that seek primarily to enhance their own welfare if they are indeed attempting to enhance their level of professionalization. Nonetheless, the question of perceptions remains open and can only be answered by saying that the faculty are considered to be more highly professionalized than many other occupation groups primarily because of the length of training required before practitioners may enter the field, and because of the necessity for certification.

The fact that becoming a teacher requires a long period of training is obvious. A master's degree for teachers in academic subject areas and equivalent trades experience for those in occupational fields certainly suggests a longer period of training than that which is required for most occupational groups. Whether teachers could perform their duties as well without such a long period of training is not a testable question—rules of certification and employment preclude such an experiment. But it does seem that the requirement of a long period of training before people can practice teaching stems from the desire by community college advocates that their institutions be considered true postsecondary or college level schools, and the certification requirements suggest the profession's desire to validate its authoritativeness. Accordingly, we expect coming years to see the community college faculty seeking higher professional status by gathering doctoral degrees that require an even longer time to obtain. Rare is the spokesman now who would say that a doctoral degree is necessary for teaching because doctoral degree holders teach better than do those with no more than master's degrees. But as an increasingly higher percentage of two-year college instructors obtain doctorates, we may soon hear this contention raised, just as it has been for so long articulated by university professors.

The formation of codes of ethics to which members of the teaching profession subscribe has not been advanced by those in two-year colleges. A code of ethics depends on a level of professional consciousness and a tendency toward self-policing, neither of which is well advanced in the two-year institutions. The terms, "help all students reach their greatest level of individual potentiality," and "provide opportunity for high quality education," and others of the type so frequently seen in the literature emanating from the two-year colleges, afford little in the way of organizing principles to which instructors might adhere.

In sum, although two-year college instructors may be moving slowly toward the development of a profession, its lines are as yet indistinct. The fact that instruction has a high level of labor intensity—that instructors insist on having close personal contact with students in classes, the smaller the better—could work to the advantage of professionalization if the faculty were about to coalesce around a definition of desired outcomes. But the fact that teaching is the only major occupation that has not developed tools that assist its average practitioners to become exceptional performers works against professionalization. The faculty do not know how to upgrade each other's skills; at most they can exhort their less worthy colleagues. More often they ignore them.

BARGAINING FOR FACULTY WELFARE AND RIGHTS

Any discussion of the professionalization of the faculty cannot ignore the development of negotiating units bargaining for faculty welfare and rights. These units put the faculty on one side of the bargaining table, the governing board and the administrators on the other, thus enhancing the split between faculty and administration that has always been more pronounced in the two-year college than the university. But that is a passing phenomenon—for decades administrators and faculty members have been at odds in the lower schools, yet the schools maintain their structure and image. More a point of concern in this discussion is that the negotiating units almost invariably bargain for welfare—wages, hours, fringe benefits, class size, and general working conditions. What has happened is that the professional associations or unions that have formed are taking the faculty away from the elements of professionalism. Not that the bargaining agents are opposed to codes of ethics, authoritative performances, and such; they tend only to address such issues in passing. Also, the unions have come to the fore just when the major national academic disciplinary associations were beginning to attend to the community colleges, hence weakening that development.

Further the rules of the bureaucracy afflict the individual. Burdened already by state, district, and institutional level requirements, the instructor turns to the professional association or union only to find more rules. With the advent of reproducible media 20 years ago and with the increase in size of most of the two-year colleges, each teacher was, in effect, given the freedom to choose how he wanted to spend his time. Did he want to continue doing all tasks, including diagnosing students, dispensing information, and preparing examinations? Or did he want to effect liaisons with his fellows, trading off certain tasks for others? Instructors are becoming less able to adjust their working conditions to suit their own predilections. The additional work rules spelled out in the negotiated agreements limit options. Work rules are almost invariably exclusionary, saying what a faculty member *cannot* be asked to do. They tend to limit the time an instructor spends on each aspect of his role, to restrict his field of action.

Unfortunately for the development of the profession, the turn toward collective bargaining came along prior to the emergence of a professional consciousness. It arose while most instructors were still attending to their duties in the manner of those who learned a craft or art during the performance of it. It came along while most instructors still held the attitude, "Why should I *read* about teaching? I *do* it all the time." It came along before the teachers tended to develop their special skills that made them uniquely teachers, as opposed to clerks, laboratory technicians, social workers, librarians, and classroom custodians.

Many philosophers have believed that a society is robbed of its moral fiber to the extent it relies on written laws. But rules breed more rules, and the process is difficult to reverse. Some administrators welcome rules that restrict their freedom of action, feeling that they are thereby protected against litigation arising from their decision. (As patriotism is the last refuge of a scoundrel, the rule book is the first refuge of the bureaucrat.) Some instructors welcome rules that suggest to them that they cannot be expected to develop their own curriculum, articulate their own objectives, or define goals for themselves and their students unless they receive extra pay.

Just as the faculty have become unified politically, they have become even more fractured conceptually. Put another way, rules that specify the amount of time an instructor must be in a classroom or on a campus suggest that the extent and quality of learning resulting from his ministrations is less important than the fact of his being present. Rules that demand an instructor be paid additional sums for committee service, media development, preparing new courses, and so on grate against the idea of professionalism. Rules protecting an instructor from being called to account by his peers or by the institutional managers for the effects of his teaching retard the development of a sense of professional responsibility. The argument that it is inconceivable that educational output can be measured is tantamount to admitting that we know the instructor should be in the classroom a specified number of hours but we have no idea of what he is supposed to be doing there.

Some commentators, perceiving the ill effects of professionalism in the university--the professors' reluctance to teach, lack of commitment to their own institution, adherence to a national reference group—applaud the retardation of professionalism in the two-year colleges. They feel that the instantly responsive institution is enhanced to the extent it can change its personnel, that a professional group protecting its own members will lead inevitably to abuses. Accordingly they suggest that the part-time faculty brought in to teach a class or two and let go when that class fails to achieve minimum enrollment is a desirable quality for a community college. They recommend as an ideal college form an institution with a corps of nonacademic managers supervising a contingent of hourly rate instructors who have no rights to their job and no expectation of continuity of contract. But even skirting the question of professionalism, the effects of a social institution comprised of people with no commitment to it or to the effects of their labors seems somehow unworthy when placed against the idea of scholars defining desired goals and value systems for client and community. At any rate, the question of the profession versus the part-time employee is being decided in another arena. Pro-rata pay will reduce the advantage an institution garners by paying part-timers at an hourly rate, and laws mandating job rights for part-timers will limit the colleges' ability to employ them as interchangeable piece workers.

The essential step that must be taken by the individual instructor who would professionalize himself in spite of national trends is to realize that the classroom is not the only place where important aspects of teaching occur. Yet, there is an essential security about the classroom. When confronted with suggestions that they take steps toward becoming more highly involved instructors performing essential organizing tasks that affect their curriculums, courses, and students, most instructors shrink away. The classroom, the departmental affiliation, the Monday-Wednesday-Friday-at-ten-two-and-four o'clock is both familiar and safe. Therein is found not only the security of salary stemming from traditional budgetary channels but also the security of knowing that no one but the teacher and his students know what is happening in there. Despite the haphazard practice of faculty "evaluation," the classroom is closed to public scrutiny.

FUTURE FACULTY ROLE CHANGES

The instructor must come out from behind the classroom door if he is to enhance his profession and his own place within it. Those who have become involved with instructional programming and the preparation of instructional media represent one pattern of coping with the environment. Others have become program heads or coordinators of satellite centers. Even so, they must take care lest the numerous demands for data, forms, and reports move them completely out of the instructional role. That has already happened to the deans of instruction who, instead of assisting their former colleagues in preparing objectives, analyzing tests, developing media, and attending to other tasks of instruction, have allowed the bureaucratic demands of the institution to consume the time they might have spent on instructional management.

The future of the faculty will inevitably see role changes. Some modifications will propel the instructor to an off-campus location. Others will allow him to stay on the campus but perform certain tasks outside the classroom. The instructor who acts as manager of a learning laboratory operates in this fashion. So does the instructor who creates programs, prepares reproducible media, or writes criteria for television presentations. Another type is the instructor who takes responsibility for coordinating the work of the part-time faculty members. He shares teaching strategies with them, monitors their courses, and coordinates their syllabi and student assessments. He sees his role as important in making certain that the course taken by the student in the evening or in the off-campus center is the same as the course taught by himself and his colleagues. Although this smacks of management or supervision rather than teaching, it need not be that way if the faculty member sees himself as magnifying his influence through assisting other instructors. Nothing in this role shift takes him further away from teaching. Quite the contrary—he magnifies his influence on students by teaching their teachers.

Some instructors have built upon their skills as lecturers to opt for large group instruction. Many of them have been successful in obtaining a variety of assistants to help them teach large groups. Yet they recognize that their managing these assistants does not make them teachers less, managers more—the management of assistance is necessary in large group instruction lest the teacher spend all his time on clerical tasks. Physicians and nurses do not mop floors and wash bedpans. Instructors who have taken this path have been forced to negotiate with their institutions for different measures of productivity. Nonetheless it can happen, and many teachers find great rewards in seeking out greater numbers of students.

Yet another role for the instructor may be stated, one that sees him moving from the classroom to be a presentor of information other than through course formats. If we consider a continuum ranging from the degree credit required course on one end, through the noncredit course and extracurricular activity, to the noncourse-related presentation on the other, we can visualize the instructor teaching in many formats. The major difference in the presentation of opportunities for learning as manifested in today's community colleges is not between academic and vocational courses but between courses and presentations that take place apart. Putting together the total of the exhibits, recitals, lectures, concerts, colloquiums, and seminars that take place under the auspices of a student activities or community service program, we see readily that much instruction takes place outside the classroom. The faculty member who is committed to his teaching can separate himself from the sanctity of the classroom and become involved in these different forms of instruction. Although many now so do, most do not; and the noncourse-related presentations, as important as they are to the instruction provided by the institution, are frequently coordinated and presented by people other than full-time faculty members.

One more role shift might be mentioned. This will see the instructor breaking away from the campus not merely to teach in a satellite center but to work in the political and social processes of the community outside the institution. Reisman has called for this type of involvement on the part of the university faculty saying, "In my own field of sociology . . . someone who does market research might be thought to have sold to commerce, and someone who enters the foreign service might be thought to have sold out to imperialism. This is cruel and self defeating snobbery. . . ." (1975, p. 19). He wants the faculty to do more than teach those who come to the campus; he sees them becoming involved in public life. Many two-year college instructors do this now by extending their disciplinary expertise to work on matters affecting their communities. The history instructor may be coordinating a local history project; the biology instructor may be working with the water control board; the automotive technology instructor may be setting up the curriculum in the local auto repair facility. All of this still falls under the heading of instruction.

Those who choose to work in the community may consider yet another pattern of relationship. The community college needs a community connection as it moves into a broader role for itself than the provision of campus-based instruction for people of the traditional college-going age group. The instructors who see this broader role for their college may choose to organize lay advisory committees who will provide a link between campus and community. Such committees may be comprised of local business people who have an interest in a particular curriculum—a vice president of the telephone company who sculpts as a hobby might be a useful member of a committee on the arts, just as the chairperson of the local historical society will prove an important member of an advisory council to the history program. The instructors who organize such committees must take care not to staff them predominantly with university professors or high school teachers in the same subject areas, lest the committee become one focusing on curriculum articulation. These committees should have a broader set of purposes: advising on the curriculum in a particular program, providing a link that can assist faculty members in placing students in jobs, helping recruit students to the program, assisting with extracurricular presentations, and, in general, supporting the program.

Lay advisory committees are well known to the occupational instructors, who recognize that they need community support. When faced with an assault on their programs, the occupational teachers tend not to say that they must be supported for who they are, or that their program should be supported because of tradition. Rather, they enlist support from their advisory committees, which can speak to the importance of the program to the community at large. The occupational instructors also use the committees for assistance in doing follow-up studies, employer surveys, and determination of the job skills to which they should orient their curriculums. The instructors of academic subjects might well take a leaf from their book.

The environment at most community colleges is not conducive to the development of the profession of teaching. Those instructors who would bring about the professionalization of their group must understand the broader aspects of the institution and act accordingly. Similarly, the environment at most community colleges does not encourage the individual instructor to step outside his classroom and address teaching in a broader context. The instructor who does so must run the risk of alienating his colleagues and face the accusation of having "sold out to the administration." Nonetheless, the instructors who see the importance of using their profession to enhance their own growth will take these risks. Those who do not stand not only to retard their own growth but also the development of their profession.

As the community colleges attract older students, part-time students, and others who traditionally have not gone to college, the faculty is forced to face a role shift. Few instructors now teach classes comprised primarily of 18- to 21-year olds. Even in the classroom a redefinition of the instructional role is being forced. In the 1950s and 1960s the introduction of reproducible media forced one type of modification in the role of the instructor. As the colleges move toward noncampus-based instruction, a further redefinition is placed before the instructor. The idea of a profession that is engaged in instruction that affects the entire community will force yet another shift. The more confident, astute, dedicated faculty members will shrug off the shortsightedness of the actions being taken ostensibly on their behalf and will move more deliberately into a broader, more important role for themselves and for the sake of their colleagues, their institution, and their community.

SUGGESTIONS FOR FUTURE GROWTH

Influential leaders in universities, two-year colleges, and state and federal agencies can do much to affect the future of the faculty. In Chapter 10 we offered recommendations for revised doctoral programs. The following is a summary of some suggestions made throughout this book, as well as additional recommendations for furthering the professionalization of the faculty and for enhancing their functioning as involved instructors.

As community-based institutions, two-year colleges must attract support for their programs from their local communities. Accordingly, the humanities must be cultivated among a lay constituency. The faculty understand the importance of community relations—nearly all survey respondents agreed with the statement "This college should be actively engaged in community service." But they do not see the community as an important asset in the humanities program. In answer to an open-ended question asking what changes the instructor would like to see effected in the humanities program, 30 percent noted "More and better humanities courses," while only 3 percent indicated "More community involvement."

Occupational programs have been quite successful in organizing interested members of the community as program advisors, student placement and recruiting agents, and program supporters. The humanities advocates should take similar action. Although the faculty generally seem disinclined to take a lead in organizing such committees, the administrators and faculty leaders should organize lay committees as advisors to the humanities programs and should involve the humanities instructors in interacting with these committees.

Humanities instructors are aware that there is a need for career programs: 38 percent agree with the statement "Career education and occupational training should be the major emphasis in today's community college." But they do not know how to bring the humanities to the students in those programs. Even though most of them think that teaching the humanities to students in occupational programs is different from teaching transfer students, they feel the former group of students should be required to take several humanities courses. The suggestion is impractical because few occupational program heads are willing to impose such a requirement.

More feasible is the insertion of portions of the humanities in otherwise technical courses. The nursing-program faculty that would not require their students to take a cultural anthropology course might welcome a three-week unit such as "The Uses of Grieving," taught by an anthropologist. The teachers of auto mechanics will not send their students to a philosophy course, but they might appreciate the philosophy instructor's preparing a course module on "Business Ethics." "The Aesthetics of Design" could be presented to students in an electronics technology program by a teacher of art. Or a classicist could teach "Greek and Latin Roots of Medical Terms" to the medical technology students.

Several obstacles to that pattern of teaching the humanities to students in occupational programs must be overcome. Most instructors are paid on the basis of classroom contact hours. Most classes are one semester long, and instructional funds are typically allocated by department. In short, the workload and budgeting formulas make it difficult for an instructor to build a section of a course to be taught to students enrolled in another course. It is essential for governing boards and administrators to revise faculty workload formulas and intramural fiscal allocations to accommodate instructors who want to teach short segments of the humanities in otherwise technical courses.

The humanities can be taught through many other means than course formats. Colloquiums, seminars, lectures, exhibits, concerts, recitals, and films are offered on most two-year college campuses for students and the lay public alike. Most of the faculty feel there are too few such extracurricular and community service presentations at their own colleges. When asked what changes in the humanities had taken place in their institution in the past seven years, only 4 percent indicated "More extracurricular courses." But when asked what changes they would like to see effected, 11 percent said they would like to see more of such activities. And 37 percent of the faculty said that if they had free choice in the matter, they would devote more time to presenting recitals or lectures outside of class.

Here again the faculty pay scales and workload formulas present an obstacle because they are based almost exclusively on the number of hours an instructor spends in the classroom, thus discouraging faculty members who would, given time, arrange extracurricular and community service presentations. District and college policies should allow released time for instructors to organize exhibits, colloquiums, seminars, and other extracurricular activities in the humanities. Extramural funding agencies can help by sponsoring workshops to teach the faculty how to integrate course work and outside class presentations.

The outside class activities in the humanities tend to be especially restricted in states where the colleges receive funds based on the number of students enrolled in courses. In nearly all institutions, the budget lines for community service and student activities differ from those received for class instruction, thus effectually separating two sets of activities that should reinforce each other. New funding formulas that run to total programmatic emphases, curricular and extracurricular, should be explored. The faculty should at least be able to draw on the student activities budget to prepare and publicize their events.

As a contribution to the study of the humanities, minority cultures should be represented, but very few minority-group members teach the humanities: 2.6 percent blacks, 1.9 percent Chicanos, less than 1 percent Asian-Americans. In colleges opened in the past five years a higher percentage of the faculty is female and/or younger than in older institutions, but ethnic minorities are not represented there to any greater degree. Overall, there is a ratio of two to one male instructors over females.

Affirmative action is not the faculty's chief concern; in fact they are strongly against preferential hiring for women and/or minority-group members at their own colleges (61 percent against, 24 percent for). Support for strict adherence to affirmative action policies comes from the part-timers with no outside employment, from the women and ethnic minorities themselves, and especially from the younger instructors. The opponents are older white males, either full-time instructors or part-timers with regular employment elsewhere. Much work must be done if the employment pattern of women and members of ethnic minorities is to be changed. Colleges may step up recruiting efforts, but the faculty serving on screening committees must want to comply with affirmative action guidelines. Each time a position is posted, the administrators should apprise the faculty of the importance to the study of the humanities of selecting minority group applicants and offer such incentives as modest budget increments to departments that recommend candidates from minority groups. The humanities instructors alone cannot overturn collegewide patterns of discrimination, but they could modify the imbalance in their own department.

As a group, the faculty have broken almost completely with the lower schools. Although half the faculty in two-year colleges have had secondary school experience, people in this group tend to be older and are not being replaced as rapidly as they once were. More to the point, few of the humanities instructors want anything to do with the secondary schools; few feel that high school teachers are useful as sources of advice on teaching. This attitude makes curriculum articulation, student recruitment, and shared instructional techniques difficult to effect between two-year colleges and secondary schools. But such activities are necessary if the two-year colleges are to act as proper entry points to postsecondary education for a majority of the high school graduates who plan to go on to college. Administrators and faculty leaders should arrange continuing series of meetings between humanities instructors at their own institution and the neighboring secondary schools, forming members of both groups into committees for articulating curriculum and instruction.

Scholarly research is not high on the list of priorities for two-year college instructors: although 61 percent of the humanities faculty say they would like to spend more time on research or professional writing, only 9 percent indicate they would "do research" if they had a free summer. The two-year institutions are uncommitted to scholarly research, and the efforts of instructors to gain support for such activities are not likely to bear fruit. Nonetheless, most of the faculty would like to have more time to plan their courses, and nearly half of them have prepared multimedia instructional programs for use in their classes. The time that is typically spent by university professors on scholarly research is properly filled in the two-year colleges by instructors developing new courses and media. Colleges should make additional resources available through faculty fellowships, instructional development grants, summer pay, and released time to encourage faculty to develop their own courses and reproducible media.

The faculty need time to learn about the latest developments in their field. Most of the respondents agree that knowledge in their field is expanding so fast that they need further training to keep up. Most want further professional development, either by enrolling in courses in a university, obtaining a higher degree, or otherwise enhancing their knowledge. Still, half feel that satisfactory opportunities for in-service training are not available at their own college.

Opportunities for further study can be presented in several ways. Fellowship programs directed toward two-year college instructors can be expanded, allowing the faculty to study at universities. Governing boards can encourage university study by offering sabbatical leaves. Yet the faculty also need to be able to study on their own campuses. State education agencies and other extramural support groups should make funds for special forms of in-service training available to the colleges directly. The faculty will make good use of properly designed programs.

The part-time instructors need their own in-service programs. They tend to be less experienced than the full-timers and to read fewer scholarly or professional journals. They are less likely to be members of professional associations and are less concerned with research, with curriculum and instruction, and with the humanities. Their work is often coordinated by an evening division dean, and the full-time faculty associate little with them. Yet, they are more likely than the full-timers to prefer further professional development. Colleges should develop in-service programs especially for the part-time instructors on their staff. And, to stimulate curriculum and instructional integration, the full-time humanities faculty should play a leading role in implementing and conducting these programs.

Two-year college faculty members have traditionally acquired a doctorate after some years on the job; that is, they do not enter the institutions holding that degree but earn it at a later time. A much higher percentage of instructors had the doctorate in 1975 than even five years earlier (14 percent as compared with 9 percent). The apparent reason is that the growth in faculty has slowed considerably. Heretofore, faculty members who attained doctorates while they were employed were balanced by the influx of new people without higher degrees; thus a constant ratio was maintained. Now that the number of *new* full-timers employed annually has dropped off considerably, the percentage of doctorate holders has become higher. Further, 24 percent of the survey respondents said they were currently working on a doctorate. If only one-fourth of these instructors get the degree by 1980, the ratio of doctorates will increase to 20 percent of the full-time faculty. Add to that the likelihood that a greater number of new full-time staff members will have doctorates, and a 22 percent total figure by 1980 is not unrealistic. In short, an even more rapid upturn in the percentage of full-time academic faculty members with doctoral degrees seems likely.

Because two-year colleges in many states operate on pay schedules that afford increments for degrees earned, people with doctoral degrees are frequently more highly paid—as much as $4,000 more per academic year in some California institutions. Yet, these faculty members seem to address their work no differently from the way their colleagues do without the degree. Doctoral degree holders are somewhat more likely to look to the university for ideas and are slightly less concerned with their students. However, they do not differ on an index of satisfaction with their work; and their concerns with curriculum and instruction and with the humanities are the same. In brief, they have already accepted the institutional mores by the time they earn the degree; and they tend not to change their attitudes or mode of functioning when they receive it.

Because these instructors are similar to nondegree holders in their orientation to teaching and to the college, the practice of awarding sizable pay increases for instructors with doctorates seems unwarranted. To avoid inordinate strain on college finances in coming years, districts should consider modifying their salary schedules to reduce or eliminate the additional stipend paid to faculty upon their receiving the doctoral degree. The funds saved should be used to support instructors who want to develop new curricular and instructional forms.

Disciplinary affiliation is weak among two-year college faculty. Many instructors teach in two or more fields, which is understandable because few colleges have enrollments large enough to support separate full-time instructors in cultural anthropology, art history, music appreciation, or cultural geography. Hence the teacher's schedule is filled out with other courses. The lack of orientation toward research, reinforced by the low rewards for doing it and by the high teaching loads, further weakens disciplinary ties. The faculty's parochialism and failure to read or write in the professional literature make it difficult for them to maintain currency in their field. As these tendencies become more marked, communication among humanities instructors on different campuses becomes less likely.

Many humanities instructors are not involved with national professional or disciplinary organizations—23 percent are not members of any professional group; 55 percent have not attended a regional or national meeting in the past three years; and 90 percent have not presented a paper. Many question the value of professional associations at all. Clearly, professional organizations have much to do in serving the two-year college instructors. Some disciplinary associations have tried, but many others have given the two-year colleges short shrift. As a minimum, they can all build programs that will appeal to that group. Further, they should launch membership drives and organize two-year college related subgroups. And because many instructors read no discipline-related journals, the colleges should provide subscriptions to journals to be placed in faculty lounges and offices.

A final set of recommendations is addressed to the graduate degree-granting institutions whose practices must be modified if they are to assist the faculty teaching the humanities—hence the humanities themselves—in two-year colleges. The graduate programs can help themselves, too, by recruiting mature, interested graduate students from the large pool of experienced faculty members.

The two-year college instructors would prefer to spend more time than they are now spending on their own graduate education, but it is difficult for them to meet the residency requirements imposed by most graduate programs. To accommodate working instructors, the graduate programs must offer courses in late afternoons and on weekends during the academic year, courses during the summer, and courses on the campuses themselves. Some programs have moved vigorously in the direction of recruiting two-year college instructors to their programs and making appropriate adjustments. The Princeton University Department of History offers a Community College Internship Program in association with Mercer County Community College. Carnegie-Mellon University has an especially designed program for two-year college history and social science instructors. The University of Michigan has a doctor of arts in the teaching of English that is directed primarily toward practicing faculty members. Several other programs might be cited, but the point is that models for restructued academic discipline-based graduate programs are available. Many more of these types of programs should be designed to accommodate faculty members who commute from two-year colleges or who can take but one or two semesters of residency.

Faculty members prefer advice on teaching that comes from their own colleagues and from their counterparts in other two-year colleges. When asked how they would rate various groups as sources of advice on teaching, 91 percent of the respondents noted that their colleagues were useful. This was the highest percent of all choices offered, ranking well ahead of "university professors." Graduate programs can capitalize on the desire of two-year college instructors to be taught by their peers by involving community college instructors as clinical professors.

Nearly half the faculty members in two-year colleges teach in two or more subject areas. This leads them to see the value of interdisciplinary courses for which they need cross disciplinary preparation programs. If interdisciplinary graduate programs cannot be readily developed, single department programs can at least be modified so graduate students are required to take substantial portions of their work in cognate areas.

The preparation of new instructors also needs some modest reshaping. Few graduate programs now require practice teaching, yet many employing administrators feel it is essential for the otherwise inexperienced applicant. The faculty, too, recognize the value of pedagogical training: when asked what type of training they would seek before teaching if they were to begin all over again, many indicated they would have preferred more student teaching and teaching methods courses. Academic departments should offer a student teaching or teaching internship component along with their traditional master of arts degree programs.

Even if all these recommendations were followed to the letter, the two-year colleges would not become centers of study in the humanities. Their mission is broader than that of the liberal arts, and nothing here suggests it should not be. Also, the faculty will not become a community of scholars banded together in the pursuit of truth, discovering new knowledge, preserving and passing on the heritage of their culture. The pattern of two-year college development will not allow it. But they need not become characterized as workers in an industrial plant concerned primarily with rights, wages, benefits, and perquisites. The ideal future for the faculty will find them defined by themselves no less than by others as a group of professionals working along with counselors, librarians, and other professional people to educate their clients and community.

American Association of Community and Junior Colleges. 1975. *Faculty in Two-Year Colleges*. Washington, D.C.: American Association of Community and Junior Colleges.

American Association for Higher Education. "Fluctuating Academic Job Scene." *College and University Bulletin* 28 (September).

Barrett, T. C. 1969. "Relationship Between Perceived Faculty Participation in the Decision-Making Process and Job Satisfaction in the Community Colleges of North Carolina." Ph.D. dissertation, North Carolina State University. Ann Arbor, Michigan: University Microfilms (70-9173).

Bayer, A. E. 1973. "Teaching Faculty in Academe: 1972-73." *ACE Research Reports* 8 (August): 1-68.

————. 1970. "College and University Faculty: A Statistical Description." *ACE Research Reports* 5 (June): 1-48.

Benewitz, M. C., Ed. 1973. National Center for the Study of Collective Bargaining in Higher Education. *Proceedings of the First Annual Conference, 1973*. New York: City University of New York (ED 086 096).*

Bloom, Michael; Norbert Ralph, and Mervin Friedman. 1973. "Patterns of Faculty Responses to Growing Student Diversity." *New Directions for Higher Education* 1 (spring): 29-48.

Brawer, F. B. 1975. *The Humanities in Two Year Colleges: The Faculty in Review*. Los Angeles, Calif.: ERIC Clearinghouse for Junior Colleges and the Center for the Study of Community Colleges (ED 111 469).

————. 1973. "Selecting and Training Teachers." *Change* 5, 56-57, 63.

————. 1971. *Values and the Generation Gap: Junior College Freshmen and Faculty*. Washington, D.C.: American Association of Junior Colleges; and Los Angeles: ERIC Clearinghouse for Junior Colleges, monograph no. 11 (ED 050 724).

————. 1968. *Personality Characteristics of College and University Faculty: Implications for the Community College*. Washington, D.C.: American Association of Junior Colleges; and Los Angeles: ERIC Clearinghouse for Junior Colleges (ED 026 048).

Bresler, Jack B. 1968. "Teaching Effectiveness and Government Awards." *Science* 169: 164-67.

Brown, James L. 1975. "Backgrounds and Characteristics of New Full-Time Community College Faculty Members." Unpublished paper, 1975. (ED 112 991).

---

*A number in parentheses, preceded by "ED," refers to an Educational Resources Information Center (ERIC) document. See page 134.

Brown, J. W., and R. C. Shukraft. 1971. "Personal Development and Professional Practice in College and University Professors." Unpublished doctoral dissertation, Graduate Theological Union. Berkeley, Calif.

Bushnell, D. S. 1973. *Organizing for Change: New Priorities for Community Colleges*. New York: McGraw-Hill.

California Education Code. 1971. Vol. 1. Sacramento: Documents Section, Department of General Services, State of California.

Cohen, Arthur M., ed. 1975a. *The Humanities in Two-Year Colleges: Reviewing Curriculum and Instruction*. Los Angeles: Center for the Study of Community Colleges and ERIC Clearinghouse for Junior Colleges (ED 110 119).

————. 1975b. *The Humanities in Two-Year Colleges: A Survey of the Faculty*. Los Angeles: Center for the Study of Community Colleges.

————, ed. 1973a. "Toward a Professional Faculty." *New Directions for Community Colleges* 1 (spring).

————. 1973b. *Work Satisfaction Among Junior College Faculty Members*. Los Angeles, Calif.: ERIC Clearinghouse for Junior Colleges (ED 081 426).

————. 1970c. "Technology: Thee or Me? Behavioral Objectives and the College Teacher." *Educational Technology* 10 (November): 57–60.

Cohen, Arthur M., et al. 1975a. "Affirmative Action Arises." In *College Responses to Community Demands: The Community College in Challenging Times*. San Francisco: Jossey-Bass, Inc.

————. 1975b. *College Responses to Community Demands: The Community College in Challenging Times*. San Francisco: Jossey-Bass, Inc.

Cross, K. P. 1969. "The Quiet Revolution." *The Research Reporter* 4: 61–64.

Dohrenwend, B. S. 1970. "An Experimental Study of Payments to Respondents." *The Public Opinion Quarterly* 34 (winter): 621–24.

Dunham, E. A. 1970. "Rx for Higher Education: The Doctor of Arts Degree." *Journal of Higher Education* 41: 505–15.

Eckert, R. E., and H. Y. Williams. 1972. *College Faculty View Themselves and Their Jobs*. Minneapolis: University of Minnesota.

Ernst, Richard J., Ed. 1975. "Adjusting to Collective Bargaining." *New Directions for Community Colleges* 3 (autumn).

Frankel, Joanne. 1973. *Junior College Faculty Job Satisfaction*. Los Angeles: ERIC Clearinghouse for Junior Colleges (ED 081 425).

Gaff, J. G. 1975. *Toward Faculty Renewal: Advances in Faculty, Instructional, and Organizational Development*. San Francisco: Jossey-Bass.

Garrison, R. H. 1967. *Junior College Faculty—Issues and Problems, A Preliminary National Appraisal*. Washington, D.C.: American Association of Junior Colleges (ED 012 177).

Guion, R. M. 1974. "Open a New Window." *American Psychologist* 29: 287–96.

Jencks, C., et al. 1972. *Inequality: A Reassessment of the Effect of Family and Schooling in America*. New York: Basic Books.

Jung, C. G. 1923. *Psychological Types*. London: Routledge & Kegan Paul.

Kelley, W., and L. Wilbur. 1970. *Teaching in the Community-Junior College*. New York: Appleton-Century-Crofts.

Kurth, E. L., and E. R. Mills. 1968. *Analysis of Degree of Faculty Satisfaction in Florida Community Junior Colleges. Final Report*. Gainesville: Florida University, Institute of Higher Education (ED 027 902).

Larson, R. 1970. *The Evaluation of Teaching College English*. New York: Modern Language Association of America.

Leslie, L. L. 1973. "Acceptance of the Community College Philosophy Among Faculty of Two-Year Institutions." *Educational Administration Quarterly* 9.

Lieberman. M. 1956. *Education as a Profession*. Englewood Cliffs, N.J.: Prentice-Hall.

Linsky, A. S. 1975. "Stimulating Responses to Mailed Questionnaires: A Review." *The Public Opinion Quarterly* 39 (spring): 82–101.

———. 1975. "Part-Time Faculty in Community Colleges." Topical Paper No. 54. Los Angeles: ERIC Clearinghouse for Junior Colleges (ED 115 316).

Many, W. A., J. R. Ellis, and P. Abrams. 1972. "In-Service Education in American Senior Colleges and Universities: A Status Report." *Illinois School Research* 8 (spring): 46–51.

Marsh, J. P., and T. Lamb, Eds. 1975 "An Introduction to the Part-Time Teaching Situation with Particular Emphasis on Its Impact at Napa Community College." Unpublished paper, 1975 (ED 125 683, available in microfilm only).

Medsker, L. L., and D. Tillery. 1971. *Breaking the Access Barriers: A Profile of Two-Year Colleges*. San Francisco: McGraw-Hill.

Millett, J. 1973. *Explorations in Undergraduate Education: Why Political Science?* New York: Carnegie Foundation for the Advancement of Teaching.

NEA Research Division. 1972. *Faculty Salary Schedules in Community Junior Colleges, 1971-72*. Washington, D.C.: National Education Association Research Division.

O'Banion, T., and J. T. Vaughn. 1975. *Emerging Models of Community College Staff Development Programs*. Urbana: University of Illinois.

Panos, R. J., and A. W. Astin. 1968. "Attrition Among College Students." *American Educational Research Journal* 5 (January): 57–72.

Park, Young. 1971. *Junior College Faculty: Their Values and Perceptions*. Monograph 12. Washington, D.C.: American Association of Junior Colleges and Los Angeles: ERIC Clearinghouse for Junior Colleges (ED 050 725).

Parsons, R. J., and T. S. Medford. 1972. "The Effect of Advance Notice in Mail Surveys of Homogeneous Groups." *The Public Opinion Quarterly* 36 (summer): 258–59.

Phair, T. S. 1975. "Changing Characteristics of Newly Employed Faculty in California Community Colleges as Perceived by Deans of Instruction." Doctoral dissertation. Berkeley: University of California (ED 126 933).

———. 1974. *Staffing Patterns in California Colleges. A 1973–74 Overview*. Sacramento: California Junior College Association (ED 087 506).

———. 1972. *Staffing Patterns in California Community Colleges. A 1972 Overview*. Berkeley: University of California (ED 070 433).

———. 1969. "Third Year Survey Results: An Analysis of the Characteristics of New Full-Time Faculty in California Community Colleges." Berkeley: Office of Educational Career Services, University of California.

Preus, Paul K., and Douglas F. Williams. 1975. "Statewide Community College Faculty Development: A Personalized Approach." Unpublished paper (ED 118 168).

Pritchett, Betty Jensen. 1973. "Values and Perceptions of Community College Professional Staff in Oregon." Doctoral dissertation, Oregon State University. Ann Arbor, Mich.: University Microfilms (73-21,321).

Purdy, Leslie N. 1973. "A Case Study of Acceptance and Rejection of Innovation by Faculty in a Community College." Doctoral dissertation, University of California, Los Angeles. Ann Arbor, Mich.: University Microfilms (74-11,563).

Riesman, David. 1975. "Can We Maintain Quality Graduate Education in a Period of Retrenchment?" Chicago: University of Illinois at Chicago Circle, Second David D. Henry Lecture.

———. 1976. "Thoughts on the Graduate Experience," *Change* 8 (April): 11–16.

Rokeach, Milton. 1968a. *Beliefs, Attitudes, and Values: A Theory of Organization and Change*. San Francisco: Jossey-Bass.

Rossmann, J. E., and A. W. Astin. 1974. "Cost-Effectiveness of Differential Techniques for Mail Questionnaires." *Research in Higher Education* 2: 273–79.

Ryan, K., Ed. 1970. *Don't Smile Until Christmas*. Chicago: University of Chicago Press.

Sewell, Donald H., et al. 1976. *Report on a Statewide Survey About Part-Time Faculty in California Community Colleges*. Sacramento: California Community and Junior College Association (ED 118 195).

Sikula, John P., Stephen G. Jurs, and Andrew F. Sikua. 1972. "Do Teachers Differ in their Values?" *Education and Urban Society* 4 (August): 459–66.

Sprenger, J. M., and R. E. Schultz. 1974. "Staff Reduction Policies." *College Management* 9 (May 4): 22–23.

Trow, M. A., Ed. 1975. *Teachers and Students: Aspects of American Higher Education.* New York: McGraw-Hill.

Walmsley, D. J. 1973. "Response Rates in Four Sydney Surveys." *Australian and New Zealand Journal of Sociology* 9 (June): 77–78.

Weingarten, S., et al. 1965. *English in Two-Year College—Report of a Joint Committee of the National Council of Teachers of English and the Conference on College Composition and Communication.* Champaign, Ill.: National Council of Teachers of English (ED 013 604).

Wilson, R. C., et al. 1975. *College Professors and Their Impact on Students.* New York: Wiley.

BIBLIOGRAPHY

American Association of Community and Junior Colleges. 1975b. *1975 Community, Junior, and Technical College Directory*. Washington, D.C.

————. 1974. *1974 Community and Junior College Directory*. Washington, D.C.

————. 1973. *1973 Community and Junior College Directory*. Washington, D.C.

American Association of Junior Colleges. 1969. *Preparing Two-Year College Teachers for the '70's: Report of a Conference (Warrenton, Virginia, November 17-29, 1968)*. Washington, D.C. (ED 034 516).*

Anderson, B. Robert. 1975. "Adjunct Faculty Deserve a Better Deal." *Change* 7 (September): 8, 64.

Association of Departments of Foreign Languages. 1971. "The Training and Orientation of Foreign Language Teachers in the Junior Colleges; A Conference report." *Bulletin of the Association of Departments of Foreign Languages* 3: 42-49.

Barton, T. L., and A. M. Beachner. 1970. *Teaching English in the Two-Year College*. Menlo Park, Calif.: Cummings.

Belford, M. L. 1967. "An Investigation and Analysis of the Public Junior College Music Curriculum with Emphasis on the Problems of the Transfer Music Major." Doctoral dissertation, University of Iowa. Ann Arbor, Michigan: University Microfilms (68-901).

Bender, Louis W., and James O. Hammons. 1972. "Adjunct Faculty: Forgotten and Neglected." *Community and Junior College Journal* 43 (October): 21-22.

Blai, B., Jr. 1972. *Values and Perceptions of a Private Junior College Faculty: Public Community College Faculties and Students*. Bryn Mawr, Pa.: Harcum Junior College (ED 061 945).

Blocker, Clyde E., Robert H. Plummer, and Richard C. Richardson, Jr. 1965. *The Two-Year College: A Social Synthesis*. Englewood Cliffs, N.J.: Prentice-Hall.

Brawer, F. B. 1974. *Three Colleges: Three Faculties*. Topical Paper no. 41. Los Angeles: ERIC Clearinghouse for Junior Colleges (ED 091 034).

————. 1973b. *New Perspectives on Personality Development in College Students*. San Francisco: Jossey-Bass.

————. 1970. *The Person: A Conceptual Synthesis*. Topical Paper no. 11. Los Angeles: ERIC Clearinghouse for Junior Colleges (ED 037 219).

---

*A number in parentheses, preceded by "ED," refers to an Educational Resources Information Center (ERIC) document. See page 134.

————. 1967. *The Concept of Ego Strength and Its Measurement Through a Word Association Technique*. Doctoral dissertation, University of California, Los Angeles. Ann Arbor, Michigan: University Microfilms (67-14, 251).

Brennan, M. J. 1970. "On the Doctor of Arts Degree." *Bulletin of the Association of Departments of Foreign Languages* 1: 52–55.

Cartter, A. M., and M. M. Salter. 1975. "Two-Year College Faculty and Enrollment Projections," In *Graduate Education and Community Colleges: Cooperative Approaches to Community College Staff Development*, S. V. Martorana et al., Eds. Technical Report No. 5. Washington, D.C.: National Board on Graduate Education (ED 111 479).

Champion, D., and A. M. Sear. 1969. "Questionnaire Response Rate: A Methodological Analysis." *Social Forces* 47 (March): 335–39.

Cohen, Arthur M. 1970a. "A Hierarchy of Disciplinarianism" Mimeographed. Los Angeles: University of California Graduate School of Education.

————. 1970b. *Objectives for College Courses*. Beverly Hills, Calif.: Glencoe Press.

————. 1969a. *Dateline '79: Heretical Concepts for the Community College*. Beverly Hills, Calif.: Glencoe Press.

————. 1969b. "Education in the Two-Year College." In *Britannica Review of American Education*, ed. D. G. Hayes, vol. 1. Chicago: Encyclopedia Britannica.

————. 1967. "Teacher Preparation: Rationale and Practice." *Junior College Journal* 37 (May): 21–25.

————. 1966. "Developing Specialists in Learning." *Junior College Journal* 37 (September): 21–23.

Cohen, Arthur M., and F. B. Brawer. 1975–76. *An Analysis of Humanities Education in Two-Year Colleges: Phase 2—The Faculty*. Los Angeles: Center for the Study of Community Colleges.

————. 1975a. *The Experimental College Responds to Demands*. Iowa City, Iowa: American College Testing; and Los Angeles: ERIC Clearinghouse for Junior Colleges.

————. 1975b. *The Humanities in Two-Year Colleges: A Review of the Students*. Los Angeles: Center for the Study of Community Colleges; and ERIC Clearinghouse for Junior Colleges (ED 108 727).

————. 1972a. *Confronting Identity: The Community College Instructor*. Englewood Cliffs, N.J.: Prentice-Hall.

————. 1972b. *The Who, What, Why of Instructor Evaluation*. Topical Paper no. 33. Los Angeles: ERIC Clearinghouse for Junior Colleges (ED 060 839).

————. 1970. *Student Characteristics; Personality and Dropout Propensity*. Washington, D.C.: American Association of Junior Colleges; and Los Angeles: ERIC Clearinghouse for Junior Colleges, monograph no. 9 (ED 038 130).

————. 1969. *Measuring Faculty Performance*. Washington, D.C.: American Association of Junior Colleges; and Los Angeles, ERIC Clearinghouse for Junior Colleges, monograph no. 4 (ED 031 222).

————. 1968. *Focus of Learning; Preparing Teachers for the Two-Year College*. Los Angeles: University of California Junior College Leadership Program (ED 019 939).

————. 1967. "Adaptive Potential and First-Year Teaching Success." *Journal of Teacher Education* 18 (summer): 179–85.

Cohen, Arthur M., and William F. Shawl. 1970. "Coordinating Instruction Through Objectives." *Junior College Journal* 41 (October): 17–19.

Cohen, Arthur M., et al. 1971. *A Constant Variable: New Perspectives on the Community College*. San Francisco: Jossey-Bass.

Cohen, Edward. 1970. "Faculty for Teaching-Learning: Proposed New Graduate Centers for the Systematic Preparation of Community College Teachers." Unpublished paper (ED 038 133).

Community College Faculty Collective Bargaining: Report and Recommendations of the Advisory Committee on Community College Faculty Collective Bargaining to the Senate Select Committee. 1975. Olympia, Wash.: Washington State Legislature (ED 111 470).

Community College Teacher Preparation. 1975. A brief prepared for the Conference on the Doctor of Arts. Los Angeles, Calif.: ERIC Clearinghouse for Junior Colleges.

Davies, T. G. "The University of Michigan's Doctor of Arts in English Program for Community College Teachers of English." Unpublished paper (ED 089 814).

Deegan, William L., et al. 1974. "Evaluating Community College Personnel: A Research Report." Unpublished paper (ED 094 847).

DeHaggard, A. Q. 1972. "The Colleges of the 80's—The Challenge to the 70's." *ADFL Bulletin* 3 (March): 27–30.

Eckert, R. E., and J. Stecklein. 1961. *Job Motivations and Satisfactions of College Teachers*. Washington, D.C.: U.S. Office of Education.

Edwards, E. A. 1971. "The Factors Which Contribute to the Effectiveness and Success of the Interrelated Humanities Course on the Sophomore Level in the Junior College." Doctoral dissertation, Florida State University. Ann Arbor, Michigan: University Microfilms (72-16583).

Erickson, A. B. 1971. "English Programs in Selected Two-Year Community Colleges, Private Liberal Arts Colleges, and State Colleges in California." Doctoral dissertation, University of Southern California. Ann Arbor, Michigan: University Microfilms (71-16407).

The Evaluation of Community College Teaching: Models in Theory and Practice. 1972. Sacramento: California Junior College Association (ED 063 923).

Fay, J. M. 1976. "Dominant Faculty Values." In *The Humanities in Two-Year Colleges: Faculty Characteristics*. Los Angeles: Center for the Study of Community Colleges; and ERIC Clearinghouse for Junior Colleges (ED 130 721).

Freedman, M., ed. 1973. *Facilitating Faculty Development: New Directions for Higher Education* 1 (spring).

Freedman, M., and M. Bloom. 1973. "Personal History and Professional Career." *New Directions for Higher Education* 1 (spring): 49–60.

Gleazer, E. J., Jr. 1967. "Preparation of Junior College Teachers." *Educational Record* 48 (spring): 147–52.

Guichard, Gus, et al. 1975. *Part-Time Employment*. Sacramento: Community Colleges Office of the Chancellor (ED 111 464, available in microfilm only).

Guidelines for the Preparation of Community/Junior College Teachers. 1968. Washington, D.C.: National Faculty Association of Community and Junior Colleges (ED 031 205).

Guth, H. P. 1970. "The Monkey on the Bicycle: Behavioral Objectives and the Teaching of English." *English Journal* 59 (September): 785–92.

Hackler, J. C., and P. Bourgette. 1973. "Dollars, Dissonance, and Survey Returns." *Public Opinion Quarterly* 37 (summer): 276–81.

Hamill, R. E. 1967. "The Effects of Teachers in Four-year Colleges and Universities as Reference Groups for Teachers in Community Colleges." Unpublished doctoral dissertation. Eugene, Oregon: University of Oregon.

Hammons, J. O., and T. H. S. Wallace. 1976. *An Assessment of Community College Staff Development Needs in the Northeastern United States*. State College, Penn.: Pennsylvania State University (ED 128 058).

Heist, P., and G. Yonge. 1962. *Omnibus Personality Inventory, Form F Manual*. New York: Psychological Corporation.

Hill, P. 1972. "Philosophy and the Two-Year Colleges." *Metaphilosophy* 3 (July): 253–60.

Hinkston, E. R. 1968. "Miseducation in History." *Improving College and University Teaching* 16 (winter): 20–22.

Kelly, M. F., and J. Connolly. 1970. *Orientation for Faculty in Junior Colleges*. Washington, D.C.: American Association of Junior Colleges; and Los Angeles: ERIC Clearinghouse for Junior Colleges, Monograph 10 (ED 043-323).

Koltai, Leslie, ed. 1975. "Merging the Humanities." *New Directions for Community Colleges* 3 (winter).

Koos, L. V. 1925. *The Junior-College Movement*. Boston: Ginn.

Lockwood, R. H. 1967. *Rationale and Design for an Interdisciplinary Humanities Course at the Community College*. Doctoral dissertation, Michigan State University. Ann Arbor, Michigan: University Microfilms (67-14520).

Lombardi, John. 1974a. *Faculty Workload*. Topical paper No. 46. Los Angeles: ERIC Clearinghouse for Junior Colleges. (ED 097 925).

————. 1974b. *Implications for Community College Governance Under Collective Bargaining*. Los Angeles: ERIC Clearinghouse for Junior Colleges (ED 086 298).

Martorana, S. V., et al., eds. 1975. *Graduate Education and Community Colleges: Cooperative Approaches to Community College Staff Development*. Technical Report, U.S. Washington, D.C.: National Board on Graduate Education (ED 111 479).

Michel, J. 1970. "Graduate Education of the Foreign Language Education Specialist." *ADFL Bulletin* 2 (December): 19–24.

Minutillo, R. G. 1972. "The Art Historian's Role in the Development of a Two-Year Liberal Arts Curriculum." Paper presented to the 60th Annual Convention of the College Art Association of America, January.

Monroe, C. R. 1972. *Profile of the Community College: A Handbook*. San Francisco: Jossey-Bass.

NEA Research Division. 1972. "Faculty Load Policies and Practices in Public Junior and Community Colleges." *Research Information for Higher Education Staff of NEA Affiliates*. Washington, D.C.: National Education Association Research Division.

1971 Junior College Directory. 1971. Washington, D.C.: American Association of Junior Colleges; and Los Angeles: ERIC Clearinghouse for Junior Colleges.

O'Banion, T. 1974. "Alternate Forms of Graduate Education for Community College Staff: A Descriptive Review." Unpublished paper (ED 100 474).

————. 1973. "Patterns of Staff Development." *New Directions for Community Colleges* 1 (spring): 9–30.

————. 1972b. *Teachers for Tomorrow; Staff Development in the Community-Junior College*. Tucson, Ariz.: University of Arizona Press.

O'Connor, E. F., Jr., and T. B. Justiz. 1970. *Identifying the Effective Instructor*. Topical Paper 9. Los Angeles: ERIC Clearinghouse for Junior Colleges (ED 035 416).

Ohren, S. H. 1972. "Approaches to the Teaching of Introductory Art History Courses in the California Community Colleges". Master's thesis. San Francisco: California State University.

Preliminary Report on Part-Time Faculty. 1975. Sacramento: California Community Colleges (ED 105 903).

Purdy, Leslie N. 1974. *Faculty in an Innovative Community College*. Topical Paper No. 45. Los Angeles: ERIC Clearinghouse for Junior Colleges (ED 094 821).

Rokeach, Milton. 1968b. "The Role of Values in Public Opinion Research." *The Public Opinion Quarterly* 32: 547–59.

Sanford, N., ed. 1962. *The American College: A Psychological and Social Interpretation of the Higher Learning*. New York: Wiley.

Savignon, S. J. 1972. "Preparation of Foreign Language Teachers for the Junior-Community College." In *Changing Patterns in Foreign Language Programs. Report of the Illinois Conference on Foreign Languages in Junior and Community Colleges, 1972*. ed. W. M. Rivers et al. Rowley, Mass.: Newbury House.

Schlesinger, Sue. H., ed. 1976. *The Humanities in Two-Year Colleges: Faculty Characteristics*. Los Angeles: Center for the Study of Community Colleges and ERIC Clearinghouse for Junior Colleges (ED 130 721).

South, James D., et al. 1975. "The Relationship of Teacher Role Orientation and Perceived Teaching Effectiveness." Paper presented at the Annual Meeting of the American Educational Research Association, Washington, D.C., March 31–April 3 (ED 104 462).

Stratton, A. G. 1969. "Needed: The Doctor of Arts in College Teaching." *Junior College Journal* 39 (May): 19–23.

Symes, K. M. 1971. "The M.A. Is Enough!" Paper presented at the Annual Meeting of the Modern Language Association, Chicago, Illinois, December (ED 073 760).

Taylor, A. 1973. "Can Community Colleges Survive the Ph.D. Glut?" Unpublished paper (ED 088 548).

Thornton, J. W., Jr. 1966. *The Community Junior College* 2d ed. New York: Wiley.

Wallace, Terry. 1974. *The Literature of Staff Development: Emphases and Shortcomings; [and] Community College Staff Development, an Annotated Bibliography*. University Park: Pennsylvania State University (ED 094 822).

Waller, Willard. 1932. *The Sociology of Teaching*. New York: Wiley.

———. 1960. "What Teaching Does to Teachers." In *Identity and Anxiety*, ed. M. Stein, A. Vidich, and D. White. New York: Free Press.

Wozniak, L. C. 1973. "A Study of the Relationship of Selected Variables and the Job Satisfaction/Dissatisfaction of Music Faculty in Two-Year Colleges." Doctoral dissertation, The Catholic University of America. Ann Arbor: University Microfilms (73-25,151).

Yarrington, Roger, Ed. 1974. *New Staff for New Students: Educational Opportunity for All. Report of the 1973 Assembly of the American Association of Community and Junior Colleges*. Washington, D.C.: American Association of Junior Colleges (ED 089 803).

The reports of the Faculty Study sponsored by the National Endowment for the Humanities have been put into the Educational Resources Information Center (ERIC) system and may be obtained on microfiche or hard copy from the ERIC Document Reproduction Service, Box 190, Arlington, Virginia 22210, or viewed in any library that has the ERIC collection.

One of the reports, Responses to the Survey, is printed here. This displays the percentages of the 1,493 humanities instructors who responded to each item on the survey form. The other reports include detailed information on how the form was developed, sample selection, and the items contained in each construct:

AN ANALYSIS OF HUMANITIES EDUCATION IN TWO-YEAR COLLEGES: PHASE II, THE FACULTY

1. What is your present principal teaching field?

	Percent
Art	6.9
Anthropology	2.8
Foreign language	14.1
History	16.5
Law/government	9.3
Liberal arts/humanities/theater	7.4
Literature	27.2
Music	6.0
Philosophy	4.7
Religious studies	2.0
Social studies/cultural geography/ethnic studies	3.1

3. Were you ever a student in a community/junior college?

	Percent
Yes	25.1
No	74.1
N/A	.7

4. At what type of school did you receive your degrees and/or certificate? (Please indicate for each degree held the type of school.)

	Associate Degree (percent)	Technical Certificate (percent)	Bachelor's Degree (percent)	Master's Degree (percent)	Doctoral Degree (percent)
Technical institute	.3	.5	.1	.3	.0
Junior/community college	11.7	.4	1.1	.8	.1
Public four-year college or university	1.1	.7	55.3	54.5	8.1
Denominational college or university	.6	.2	22.6	11.7	1.7
Private, nonsectarian college or university	.4	.4	17.3	21.9	5.6
Other	.5	.4	.8	.7	.3

5./6. What was your graduate major(s)?

	Percent		Percent
Agriculture/forestry	.1	Liberal arts	2.1
Architecture/graphics	.3	Life sciences	.3
Art	6.9	Linguistics	1.7
Anthropology	1.7	Literature	30.4
Business	.4	Mathematics	.2
Criminology	.3	Music	7.3
Education	14.4	Nursing	.1
Engineering	.1	Philosophy	4.5
Foreign language	12.1	Physical education	.5
Geography	1.1	Physical sciences	.3
Guidance/counseling	1.1	Political science	8.4
Health	.1	Psychology	1.5
History	18.8	Religious studies	3.5
Industrial arts	.1	Social sciences	4.6
Law	1.3	Speech/drama	3.8
		Human services/ social work	.2
		Basic studies/communications	.1

7. Toward what kind of degree are you currently working?

	Percent		Percent
Associate degree	.2	Master's degree	7.0
Technical degree	.6	Doctoral degree	23.6
Bachelor's degree	.4	None	68.1

8. Your sex:

	Percent
Female	33.3
Male	66.7

9. Your age:

	Percent
Under 25	1.3
26–30	12.1
31–35	20.3
36–40	16.2
41–45	13.1
46–50	13.8
51–55	9.5
56–60	7.6
61 and older	6.2

10. Are you:

	Percent
White/Caucasian	90.6
Black/Negro/Afro-American	2.6
American Indian	.2
Oriental	.9
Mexican-American/Chicano	1.9
Puerto Rican-American	.3
Other	1.9
N/A	1.5

11. About how many books were there in the home in which you were raised?

1–10	11–25	26–100	101–200	Over 200	No Answer
6.4	9.8	25.7	19.0	38.3	.8

12. How many years were you an instructor or an administrator	None	Less Than One Year	1–2 Yrs.	3–4 Yrs.	5–10 Yrs.	11–20 Yrs.	Over 20 Yrs.	N/A
				(percent)				
in a secondary school?	41.1	3.5	10.4	10.4	17.7	8.8	2.3	5.7
in a four-year college or university (beyond the level of teaching or research assistant)?	54.7	3.1	11.6	7.6	9.4	4.0	1.1	8.4
13. Within any two-year college how many years have you been								
a faculty member?	3.6	7.3	13.4	16.3	37.7	16.7	3.8	1.2
a department or division chairperson?	66.8	2.6	7.2	5.2	6.0	1.6	.5	10.0
the director of a special program (such as remedial studies, ethnic studies)?	80.7	1.5	2.3	1.9	1.1	.1	—	12.5
an administrator (such as dean, president)?	83.7	.3	1.3	1.0	1.0	.3	.1	12.3

14. Are you currently the chairperson of your division or department?

	Percent
Yes	14.9
No	83.7
N/A	1.3

(If yes, answer a–e)

a. Have you employed people with doctorate degrees as instructors in your department or division?

	Percent
Yes	47.5
No	49.3
N/A	3.1

b. Has there been pressure from other administrators and/or from the faculty

	Percent
to hire people with a doctorate?	4.9
not to hire people with a doctorate?	4.5
no pressure either way.	87.0
N/A	3.1

c. In the future do you plan to hire instructors who hold a doctoral degree?

	Percent
Yes	61.4
No	24.2
N/A	14.3

d. Why?

	Percent
Hire the best person regardless of degree	29.6
More capable/knowledgeable	15.7
Best qualified candidate	7.2
Prestige/up-grade faculty	2.7
If available we hire them	1.8
Teachers required by accrediting association to hold doctorate	1.3

Why not?

Want higher salary	8.5
Degree not necessary to teach in my department	6.3
Not enough practical experience	3.1
Too specialized to meet needs of two-year college	1.8

	Percent
They are not available	1.8
Too research-oriented	.9
All others	3.1
Don't know/no answer	11.2

e. What has been your experience with instructors holding the doctorate?

	Percent
They are fine teachers	24.2
Their performance is the same as others	22.0
I have no experience	15.1
They are good leaders/ have high professional qualities	10.3
They have good personal qualities	2.2
They do not know how to teach	6.7
They are unable to relate to students	6.7
A negative experience—they are too high thinking	4.9
They are too ambitious	1.3
All others	.9
N/A	19.7

15. How may years have you worked in your current institution?

	None or Less Than One Year	1–2 Yrs.	3–4 Yrs.	5–10 Yrs.	11–20 Yrs.	Over 20 Yrs.	N/A
Percent	9.6	13.5	17.0	42.1	14.9	2.3	.5

16. How many class hours a week are you teaching this term?

	None	3 or Less	4–6 Hrs.	7–9 Hrs.	10–12 Hrs.	13–15 Hrs.	15–18 Hrs.	More Than 18 Hrs.
Percent	1.9	8.5	10.7	8.2	17.1	32.1	13.2	8.2

17. Are you considered to be a full-time faculty member?

	Percent
Yes	75.6
No	23.5
N/A	.9

18. a. Are you currently employed in a job in addition to your position at this college?

	Percent
Yes	26.4
No	72.9
N/A	.7

(If "yes"):

b. How many hours per week?

	1–10	11–20	21–30	31–40	More Than 40	N/A
Percent	35.5	16.8	10.4	24.4	11.9	1.0

19. How would you rate each of the following

	Excellent (percent)	Good (percent)	Fair (percent)	Poor (percent)	N/A (percent)
a. Your salary	11.1	44.1	32.2	11.7	.9
b. Relations with colleagues	41.2	50.5	6.5	1.0	.8
c. Relations with students	58.2	39.1	2.0	–	.7
d. Relations with administrators	30.2	48.6	16.0	4.5	.7
e. Relations with family and friends	64.2	32.6	2.0	.1	.9
f. Job security	28.8	43.4	15.2	11.7	.9
g. Opportunities to be creative	33.1	41.9	19.0	5.1	.9
h. Feelings about living up to your greatest potential	17.3	49.3	25.2	6.8	1.4
i. Your degree of autonomy	28.8	50.8	15.8	3.1	1.5
j. Freedom to choose textbooks, programs, and media in your area	53.2	32.1	10.2	3.8	.6
k. Your students' enthusiasm for learning	11.8	47.5	33.9	5.5	1.3
l. Your working environment in general	16.1	57.2	22.0	4.0	.7
m. Your life in general	35.7	55.7	6.2	.7	1.7

20. Please respond to the following questions by marking the appropriate space:

	Yes (percent)	No (percent)	N/A (percent)
a. Where you ever a teaching assistant in a four-year college or university?	39.4	59.4	1.2
b. Did you ever do a student teaching assignment in a two-year college?	6.0	92.7	1.3
c. Have you ever received a formal award for outstanding teaching?	20.8	77.8	1.4
d. Have you taught courses jointly with faculty members outside your department?	27.1	71.9	1.0
e. Have you ever had an article published in a journal in your field?	29.0	69.9	1.1
f. In the past three years did you go off campus to attend a conference or symposium related to teaching?	76.1	22.7	1.2
g. Do you use a syllabus for teaching your courses?	72.8	25.6	1.6
h. Have you ever been a paid consultant?	32.5	66.2	1.3
i. Have you revised your syllabus and/or teaching objectives in the past three years?	92.7	5.0	2.3
j. Do you sometimes run an item analysis on a test that you give your students?	49.8	46.7	3.5
k. Do you usually distribute sets of written measurable objectives to your students?	47.4	50.0	2.5
l. Have you authored or coauthored a published book?	12.5	86.2	1.3
m. Have you ever applied to an outside agency for a research grant to study a problem in your field?	24.6	74.3	1.1
n. Have you ever prepared a replicable or multimedia instructional program for use in your classes?	41.5	56.4	2.1
o. Do you typically submit written evidence of student learning (other than grade marks) to your dean or department head?	16.9	81.4	1.7
p. Since you have been teaching have you ever received a stipend or grant from your own college (such as faculty fellowship)?	16.3	79.8	3.9
a private foundation (such as Ford, Danforth), or a professional association?	7.8	85.1	7.2
state or federal government agency (such as National Endowment for the Humanities)?	16.9	77.5	5.6

21. How would you rate the following as sources of advice on teaching?

	Quite Useful (percent)	Some-what Useful (percent)	Not Very Useful (percent)	N/A (percent)
Department chairpersons	30.4	38.6	26.9	4.0
University professors	21.0	45.5	28.8	4.6
Colleagues	52.9	38.4	6.4	2.2
High school teachers	10.7	35.2	47.2	6.9
Students	43.3	46.3	8.0	2.5
Administrators	8.2	33.4	54.3	4.1
Professional journals	24.4	51.5	20.8	3.3
Programs of professional associations	17.7	49.7	28.9	3.8

22. How many journals or periodicals do you subscribe to and/or read regularly or occasionally?

	Discip-line Related (percent)	Profes-sional Educa-tional (percent)	General Inter-est (percent)
None	25.7	63.9	78.4
One	20.1	22.6	11.5
Two	20.4	8.4	5.2
Three	15.7	3.4	2.2
Four	8.8	1.2	1.8
Five	4.6	.5	.6
Six	2.9	.1	.2
Seven or more	1.8	—	.1

23. If you had free choice in the matter, how much time would you give the following?

	More Than Now (percent)	Same Amount (percent)	Less Than Now (percent)	N/A (percent)
Classroom instruction	28.7	55.5	13.7	2.1
Your own graduate education	52.7	37.5	3.5	6.3
Research or professional writing	61.0	32.0	3.7	3.3
Administrative activities	8.4	48.6	36.9	6.1
Professional association work	16.5	65.0	13.2	5.3
Community service	30.7	61.0	5.3	3.0
Personal affairs	42.6	52.8	1.9	2.7
Student interaction outside class	48.9	47.4	1.5	2.1
Conferring with colleagues	41.4	53.4	2.9	2.3
Reading student papers or tests	13.1	66.9	17.6	2.4
Planning instruction	47.1	48.4	2.4	2.1
Presenting recitals or lectures outside of class	37.0	52.8	6.2	4.1

24. On your most recent working day how many hours did you spend in:

	0–1	1+	2+	3+	4+	5+ (percent)	6+	7+	8+	9+	10+
a. Classroom instruction	4.3	5.0	12.6	39.0	18.8	10.4	5.1	1.7	1.3	0.6	1.2
b. Your own graduate education	81.1	7.4	5.4	3.5	0.9	0.7	0.5	0.1	0.1	–	0.3
c. Research or professional writing	73.1	10.6	9.6	3.2	1.7	0.9	0.3	0.1	0.1	0.1	0.4
d. Administrative activities (including committee work)	48.2	26.3	13.0	5.0	2.7	1.7	1.4	0.7	0.6	0.1	0.3
e. Professional association work	89.4	7.3	2.0	0.7	0.3	0.2	0.1	–	0.1	–	–
f. Community service	74.1	14.9	6.7	2.9	0.6	0.2	0.2	0.2	0.1	–	0.1
g. Personal affairs	32.3	16.3	20.1	12.3	7.8	4.0	2.5	0.8	1.7	0.3	1.9
h. Student interaction outside class	36.9	38.7	17.3	5.0	1.4	0.3	0.3	–	0.1	–	–
i. Informal interaction with colleagues	46.7	43.3	7.8	1.5	0.3	0.1	0.1	–	–	–	0.2
j. Reading student papers or tests	39.2	27.6	21.0	6.8	2.7	1.7	0.6	0.1	0.1	–	0.1
k. Planning instruction	27.5	35.4	25.2	7.5	2.4	1.0	0.7	–	0.1	–	0.1

25a. Would you like to take steps toward professional development in the next five years?

	Percent
Yes	85.9
No, I've gone as far as I can	12.9
N/A	1.2

If "yes":

b. Which of the following most appeals to you?

	Percent
Enroll in courses in a university	32.4
Ph.D. or Ed.D.	33.8
Doctor of arts	6.7
Masters degree	7.6
Enroll in in-service courses at your college	9.4
Other	20.0
N/A	.7

26. If you had a free summer, what would you do with it?

	Percent
Travel	52.8
Take classes/read/study	33.3
Recreation/rest	17.4
Write for publication	14.1
Do research	8.7
Work on advanced degree	8.2
Create/perform/paint	7.6
Work as teacher/prepare classes	6.5
Attend professional workshops	1.7
Work at trade	1.3
All other	.2
N/A	3.9

27. What type of training would you seek before teaching if you were to begin all over again?

	Percent
Do the same	33.2
Study humanities	11.6
Do more student teaching	9.2
Take more teaching methods courses	9.1
Get higher degree	5.8
Take more psychology/developmental courses	5.6

	Percent
Acquire business/technical skills	4.6
Study social science	3.3
Go to law or medical school	3.0
Take fewer education courses	2.4
Less emphasis on specialized training	2.3
Study math or science	1.9
Prepare for community college	1.1
Not teach	1.1
Go to a different college	1.0
Would not get higher degree	.1
All others	4.8
No answer	11.5

28. Five years from now you might be considering the following positions. How attractive do they appear to you at this time?

	Very Attractive (percent)	Somewhat Attractive (percent)	Un-attractive (percent)	N/A (percent)
A faculty position at a four-year college or university	39.0	36.2	18.8	6.0
A faculty position at another community or junior college	20.5	40.8	32.0	6.7
An administrative position in a community or junior college	13.7	24.4	55.2	6.7
A position in a professional association	5.5	24.7	62.7	7.1
A school outside the United States	22.7	37.9	32.6	6.8
Any position but this college	4.0	18.6	66.2	11.2
A nonteaching, non-academic position	7.6	25.3	59.3	7.8
I would be doing what I'm doing now	37.9	40.2	14.4	7.5
I have no idea	4.7	8.8	47.4	39.2

29. What has been your affiliation with professional organizations in the past three years?

	None	One	Two	Three	Four	Five	Six	Seven
				(percent)				
Member	22.5	27.1	23.9	15.9	7.6	2.1	.6	.3
Attended a regional/national meeting	54.9	24.2	12.9	5.9	1.7	.3	.1	—
Presented a paper	90.4	8.1	.9	.3	.2	—	.1	—

30. How would you rate the qualities that students should gain from a two-year college education?

	Very Important (percent)	Less Important (percent)	N/A (percent)
a. Knowledge and skill directly applicable to their careers	76.9	21.0	2.1
b. An understanding and mastery of some academic discipline	63.6	34.2	2.3
c. Preparation for further formal education	80.4	17.5	2.1
d. Self-knowledge and a personal identity	89.0	9.2	1.7
e. Aesthetic awareness	76.8	21.1	2.1
f. Knowledge of and interest in community and world problems	83.3	14.9	1.9

31. How many humanities courses do you think students in two-year occupational programs should be required to take?

	None	One	Two	Three	Four	Five	Six or More	No Opinion
Percent	1.7	2.1	10.7	13.2	22.4	9.1	34.6	6.1

32. The humanities can be offered through other than course-related presentation. Do you think there are too few, sufficient, or too many of these activities open to students at your college?

	Too Few (percent)	Suffi- cient (percent)	Too Many (percent)	Don't Know—N/A (percent)
a. Colloquiums and seminars	69.3	18.1	.9	11.7
b. Lectures	51.7	35.9	4.2	8.2
c. Exhibits	56.6	33.9	.8	8.7
d. Concerts and recitals	54.9	36.3	.8	8.0
e. Films	41.7	45.9	4.4	8.0

33. How do you experience the humanities other than through your teaching?

	Percent
Visit museums/concerts/theater	58.6
Read	50.0
Records/television/radio	21.0
Attend classes/lectures/seminars	18.6
Participate in fine arts groups	15.7
Everyday experience	15.5
Talk with peers	14.9
Travel	14.1
Community service/church work	9.8
All others	.3
N/A	12.1

34. What changes in humanities have taken place at your college in the past seven years?

	Percent
Added/improved humanities courses	29.1
Improved facilities/materials	6.4
Integrated humanities into interdisciplinary courses	5.5
More emphasis on individual development/seminars	4.3
Improved teaching techniques	4.1
More extracurricular courses	4.0
More student interest	3.3
Added ethnic studies	2.5
Better teachers	1.6
Added/improved social science courses	1.4
More student participation in program planning	1.0
Lowered standards to meet needs of slower students	.6

	Percent
Improve teaching conditions	.6
All other positive changes	1.7
Fewer humanities courses	4.6
Deemphasis of importance	3.0
Lowered standards	1.9
Decline in student interest	1.5
Lowered required number of courses	1.3
Drop in dollar support	.5
Little or no change	10.9
All other negative changes	.8
No answer	31.8

35. What changes would you like to see effected?

	Percent
Added/improved humanities courses	30.1
Integrated humanities into interdisciplinary courses	13.9
More extracurricular courses	10.6
Improved facilities/materials	7.4
More emphasis on individual development/seminars	6.5
Improved teaching techniques	5.0
More student interest courses	4.1
Improve teaching conditions	3.8
More administrative support for humanities	3.8
More community involvement	3.0
Reemphasize basic skills	3.0
More student interest/respect for the humanities	2.7
Better teachers	1.8
Added/improved social science	1.7
Added ethnic studies	1.5
More student participation in program planning	1.5
More freedom in instruction	1.3
Reinstate former program	.8
Lowered standards for slower students	.7
Special courses for vocational-technical teachers	.3
All other positive changes	5.0
All other negative changes	.2
No answer	26.7

36.   How do you feel about the following?

	Strongly Agree	Somewhat Agree	Don't Know or No Opinion (in percent)	Somewhat Disagree	Strongly Disagree
a. Overall, this institution's administration is creative and effective	17.1	38.6	10.4	19.1	14.7
b. This college should be actively engaged in community services	60.6	30.1	5.6	2.9	.7
c. Most faculty members should take some type of academic course work or engage in a creative activity (such as writing a book) at least every three years	38.0	34.1	9.6	12.3	5.4
d. Teaching the humanities to students in occupational and remedial programs is different from teaching transfer students	31.6	38.6	13.6	10.8	5.2
e. I feel considerable personal strain in my commitments to different aspects of my job	15.5	28.3	12.5	23.0	20.7
f. It is as important for a person to experience his emotions and feelings as it is to develop his intellectual or cognitive skills	52.2	31.8	7.1	6.8	2.1

	Strongly Agree	Somewhat Agree	Don't Know or No Opinion (in percent)	Somewhat Disagree	Strongly Disagree
g. All too often the present is filled with unhappiness. It's only the future that counts.	1.8	4.8	9.8	23.9	59.8
h. Collective bargaining by faculty members has a definite place in a community college	43.1	25.1	17.1	9.1	5.6
i. I believe that if I work hard, things will work out for me	25.9	47.0	13.1	10.6	3.5
j. Faculty members in all kinds of higher education institutions should engage in a process of self-evaluation	67.9	25.6	4.4	1.5	.5
k. Career education and occupational training should be the major emphasis in today's community college	11.0	26.6	8.6	34.1	19.7
l. Most humanities instructors are well prepared to teach	7.8	35.6	30.4	21.0	4.9
m. Growth is a never-ending process and should be a continuous quest	88.0	7.8	3.3	.7	.3
n. Exciting developments are taking place in the humanities	38.9	33.6	18.3	7.9	1.3

	Strongly Agree	Somewhat Agree	Don't Know or No Opinion	Somewhat Disagree	Strongly Disagree
			(in percent)		
o. The humanities are being diminished in importance in the community college	21.6	37.8	22.2	13.5	5.0
p. Satisfactory opportunities for inservice training are not available at this college	20.4	28.5	24.8	18.6	7.6
q. As a child I felt especially proud of my mother, father, or other member of my family	53.7	28.3	8.4	7.8	1.7
r. Teaching effectiveness should be the primary basis for faculty promotion	43.6	40.5	7.8	6.2	1.9
s. Faculty promotions should be based in part on formal student evaluations of their teachers	20.7	41.6	8.4	19.0	10.3
t. Faculty should engage in more interdisciplinary courses	34.7	44.9	14.1	4.8	1.5
u. I would like to have closer contacts with university faculty members who teach the same course I teach	36.9	41.9	14.5	5.2	1.5
v. The administration of my department is not very democratic	9.0	12.3	18.2	24.4	36.2

	Strongly Agree	Somewhat Agree	Don't Know or No Opinion	Somewhat Disagree	Strongly Disagree
			(in percent)		
w. I prefer to teach small classes	43.5	36.0	8.0	10.4	2.0
x. Claims of discriminatory practices against women and minority students in higher education have been greatly exaggerated	10.9	23.9	19.4	23.9	21.8
y. I tend to pattern my teaching after my own college or university courses	6.1	37.2	4.6	31.9	20.2
z. There should be preferential hiring for women and/or minority faculty at this institution	7.1	16.1	15.9	29.9	31.0
aa. If I had a chance to retrace my steps, I would not choose an academic life	2.9	5.9	10.3	20.0	60.9
bb. Knowledge in my field is expanding so fast that I need further training in order to keep up	14.4	41.2	8.0	28.2	8.2
cc. Compared with most people of my age in my field who have had comparable training, I have been more successful	13.8	36.2	35.2	12.3	2.5
dd. Students should not have representation on the governing boards of colleges and universities	5.4	12.3	9.0	36.9	36.4

	Strongly Agree	Somewhat Agree	Don't Know or No Opinion	Somewhat Disagree	Strongly Disagree
			(in percent)		
ee. Most of the important ideas about the humanities come from the university	6.3	22.0	24.0	31.7	16.0
ff. The same humanities courses should be given to humanities and nonhumanities students (such as occupational students, science majors)	19.4	33.2	11.0	30.0	6.4
gg. Time hangs heavy on my hands when I am not teaching or acting as a college administrator	3.4	6.0	7.2	17.3	66.0
hh. The humanities curriculum in my college should be modified	13.6	35.0	30.9	14.1	6.3

37. People often feel differently with different groups and in different situations. Which figure or figures in the boxes below best describe how you see yourself in relation to the different groups listed? (You may choose the same figure or different figures for your responses. Please mark one box in each row.)

	Fig. A	Fig. B	Fig. C	Fig. D	Fig. E	Fig. F	N/A
			(percent)				
Other instructors in my field	9.2	32.4	32.6	3.5	2.3	9.7	10.3
Most instructors at this school	13.3	27.1	29.4	4.1	4.5	11.7	9.9
My family	4.7	29.2	42.5	5.8	1.2	6.2	10.4

	Fig. A	Fig. B	Fig. C	Fig. D	Fig. E	Fig. F	N/A
My group of friends	3.8	28.1	47.7	.5	1.3	8.6	10.0
Teacher organizations	19.0	18.6	12.3	6.4	16.7	12.5	13.7
My students	12.7	21.3	30.3	18.2	5.0	2.6	9.8
College administrators	21.5	17.7	12.9	6.5	24.4	6.8	10.2

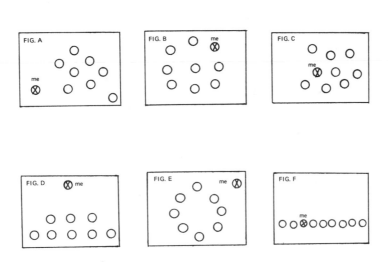

38. Below is a list of 18 values* arranged in alphabetical order. We are interested in finding out the relative importance of these values to *you*. Study the list carefully and pick out the one value which is the most important for you. Place a *1* on the blank line to the left of this value and cross it off your list. Look at the remaining 17 values; which is *second* most important for you? Place a 2 next to this value and cross it off your list. Look at the remaining 16 values and rank them in order of importance. The value which is *least* important should be ranked 18th.

---

*Rokeach Terminal Values Scale (Rokeach, 1968a).

Median	Rank	
12.76	14	A comfortable life (a prosperous life)
9.97	11	Equality (brotherhood, equal opportunity for all)
9.89	10	An exciting life (a stimulating, active life)
5.58	4	Family security (taking care of loved ones)
6.12	5	Freedom (independence, free choice)
6.71	7	Happiness (contentedness)
5.00	3	Inner harmony (freedom from inner conflict)
6.74	8	Mature love (sexual and spiritual intimacy)
15.25	17	National security (protection from attack)
13.57	16	Pleasure (an enjoyable, leisurely life)
16.16	18	Salvation (saved, eternal life)
4.23	1	Self-respect (self-esteem)
6.39	6	A sense of accomplishment (lasting contribution)
12.96	15	Social recognition (respect, admiration)
7.68	9	True friendship (close companionship)
4.78	2	Wisdom (a mature understanding of life)
10.52	12	A world at peace (free of war and conflict)
10.97	13	A world of beauty (beauty of nature and the arts)

CENTER FOR THE STUDY OF COMMUNITY COLLEGES

Your college is participating in a national study conducted by the Center for the Study of Community Colleges under a grant from the National Endowment for the Humanities. The study is concerned with the role of the humanities in two-year colleges — how they are taught by faculty, understood by students, and supported by administrators.

The survey asks a variety of questions concerning your background, experiences, and attitudes. All information is treated as confidential and at no time will your answers be singled out. Our concern is with aggregate views as discerned in a nationwide sample.

We recognize that some of the survey items cannot readily be answered "Yes" or "No." However, please respond according to your own best judgment. We recognize also that the survey is time-consuming and we appreciate your taking time to complete it.

Thanks very much for your efforts.

1. What is your present principal teaching field? _____ 11-1
   12-13

2. Your department or division of teaching appointment? _____ 14-15

3. Were you ever a student in a community/junior college?   YES ☐ 1   NO ☐ 2   16

4. At what type of school did you receive your degrees and/or certificate? (Please indicate for each degree held the type of school and the year in which it was obtained.)

	ASSOCIATE DEGREE	TECHNICAL CERTIFICATE	BACHELORS DEGREE	MASTERS DEGREE	DOCTORAL DEGREE
	17	18	19	20	21
TECHNICAL INSTITUTE	☐ 1	☐ 1	☐ 1	☐ 1	☐ 1
JUNIOR/COMM. COLLEGE	☐ 2	☐ 2	☐ 2	☐ 2	☐ 2
PUBLIC FOUR-YEAR COLLEGE OR UNIVERSITY	☐ 3	☐ 3	☐ 3	☐ 3	☐ 3
DENOMINATIONAL COLLEGE OR UNIVERSITY	☐ 4	☐ 4	☐ 4	☐ 4	☐ 4
PRIVATE, NON-SECTARIAN COLLEGE OR UNIVERSITY	☐ 5	☐ 5	☐ 5	☐ 5	☐5
OTHER (Specify)	_____	_____	_____	_____	_____
YEAR OBTAINED	year 22-23	year 24-25	year 26-27	year 28-29	year 30-31

5. Your graduate major (or majors) ? _____ 32-33

6. Major of highest graduate degree now held? _____ 34-35

7. Toward what kind of degree are you currently working?

   ASSOCIATE DEGREE   ☐ 1   BACHELORS   ☐ 3   DOCTORAL DEGREE   ☐ 5   36
   TECHNICAL CERTIFICATE ☐ 2   MASTERS   ☐ 4   NONE   ☐ 6

8. Your sex: MALE ☐ 1   FEMALE ☐ 2   37

9. Year of birth _____   38-39

10. Are you: WHITE/CAUCASIAN   □1   MEXICAN-AMERICAN/CHICANO   □5   40
               BLACK/NEGRO/AFRO-AMERICAN □2   PUERTO RICAN-AMERICAN   □6
               AMERICAN INDIAN   □3   OTHER   □7
               ORIENTAL   □4

11. About how many books were there in the home in which you were raised?

      1 - 10 □1   11 - 25 □2   26 - 100 □3   101 - 200 □4   OVER 200 □5   41

	NONE	LESS THAN ONE YEAR	1-2 YRS.	3-4 YRS.	5-10 YRS.	11-20 YRS.	OVER 20 YRS	
12. How many years were you an instructor or an administrator								
. . . in a secondary school?	□1	□2	□3	□4	□5	□6	□7	42
. . . in a four-year college or university (beyond the level of teaching or research assistant?	□1	□2	□3	□4	□5	□6	□7	43
. . .								
13. Within any two-year college how many years have you been								
. . . a faculty member?	□1	□2	□3	□4	□5	□6	□7	44
. . . a department or division chairperson?	□1	□2	□3	□4	□5	□6	□7	45
. . . the director of a special program (e.g. Remedial Studies, Ethnic Studies)?	□1	□2	□3	□4	□5	□6	□7	46
. . . an administrator (e.g. Dean, President)?	□1	□2	□3	□4	□5	□6	□7	47

14. Are you currently the chairperson of your   YES □1   (If you are chairperson of your division or department,   48
    division or department?   NO □2   please answer questions below otherwise skip to
                                                                  Question 15 on next page.)

a. Have you employed people with doctor-   d. Why?   -52-53
   ate degrees as instructors in your depart- YES □1   49
   ment or division?   NO □2

b. Has there been pressure from other administrators   e. What has been your experience with instructors   54-55
   and/or from the faculty . . .   holding a doctorate? (Please describe)
   TO HIRE PEOPLE WITH A DOCTORATE   □1   50
   NOT TO HIRE PEOPLE WITH A DOCTORATE □2
   NO PRESSURE EITHER WAY   □3

c. In the future do you plan to hire instructors
   who hold a doctoral degree?   YES □1   51
                                      NO □2

	NONE OR LESS THAN ONE YEAR	1-2 YRS.	3-4 YRS.	5-10 YRS.	11-20 YRS.	OVER 20 YRS.	

15. How many years have you worked in your current institution?   □1 □2 □3 □4 □5 □6   56

16. How many class hours a week are you teaching this term _____ HOURS A WEEK   57-58

17. Are you considered to be a full-time faculty member?   YES □1   NO □2   59

18.a Are you currently employed in a job in addition to your position at this college?   YES □1   NO □2   60

(If "yes"): b. How many hours per week?
   1-10 □1   11-20 □2   21-30 □3   31-40 □4   MORE THAN 40 □5   61

19. How would you rate each of the following

		EXCELLENT	GOOD	FAIR	POOR	
a.	Your salary	□1	□2	□3	□4	62
b.	Relations with colleagues	□1	□2	□3	□4	63
c.	Relations with students	□1	□2	□3	□4	64
d.	Relations with administrators	□1	□2	□3	□4	65
e.	Relations with family and friends	□1	□2	□3	□4	66
f.	Job security	□1	□2	□3	□4	67
g.	Opportunities to be creative	□1	□2	□3	□4	68
h.	Feelings about living up to your greatest potential	□1	□2	□3	□4	69
i.	Your degree of autonomy	□1	□2	□3	□4	70
j.	Freedom to choose textbooks, programs and media in your area	□1	□2	□3	□4	71
k.	Your students' enthusiasm for learning	□1	□2	□3	□4	72
l.	Your working environment in general	□1	□2	□3	□4	73
m.	Your life in general	□1	□2	□3	□4	74

20.   Please respond to the following questions by marking the appropriate space:

		YES	NO	
a.	Were you ever a teaching assistant in a four-year college or university?	☐1	☐2	12
b.	Did you ever do a student teaching assignment in a two-year college?	☐1	☐2	13
c.	Have you ever received a formal award for outstanding teaching?	☐1	☐2	14
d.	Have you taught courses jointly with faculty members outside your department?	☐1	☐2	15
e.	Have you ever had an article published in a journal in your field?	☐1	☐2	16
f.	In the past three years did you go off campus to attend a conference or symposium related to teaching?	☐1	☐2	17
g.	Do you use a syllabus for teaching your courses?	☐1	☐2	18
h.	Have you ever been a paid consultant?	☐1	☐2	19
i.	Have you revised your syllabus and/or teaching objectives in the past three years?	☐1	☐2	20
j.	Do you sometimes run an item analysis on a test that you give your students?	☐1	☐2	21
k.	Do you usually distribute sets of written measurable objectives to your students?	☐1	☐2	22
l.	Have you authored or co-authored a published book?	☐1	☐2	23
m.	Have you ever applied to an outside agency for a research grant to study a problem in your field?	☐1	☐2	24
n.	Have you ever prepared a replicable or multi-media instructional program for use in your classes?	☐1	☐2	25
o.	Do you typically submit written evidence of student learning (other than grade marks) to your dean or department head?	☐1	☐2	26
p.	Since you have been teaching have you ever received a stipend or grant from . . . . . . your own college (e.g. faculty fellowship)?	☐1	☐2	27
	. . . a private foundation (e.g. Ford, Danforth), or a professional association?	☐1	☐2	28
	. . . state or federal government agency (e.g. National Endowment for the Humanities)?	☐1	☐2	29

21. How would you rate the following as sources of advice on teaching?

	QUITE USEFUL	SOME-WHAT USEFUL	NOT VERY USEFUL	
Department Chairpersons	☐1	☐2	☐3	30
University Professors	☐1	☐2	☐3	31
Colleagues	☐1	☐2	☐3	32
High School Teachers	☐1	☐2	☐3	33
Students	☐1	☐2	☐3	34
Administrators	☐1	☐2	☐3	35
Professional Journals	☐1	☐2	☐3	36
Programs of Professional Organizations	☐1	☐2	☐3	37

22. Which professional journals or periodicals do you subscribe to and/or read regularly or occasionally? (List below and indicate which ones you subscribe to, which ones you read regularly, and which ones you read occasionally.)

	SUBSCRIBE TO	READ REGULARLY	READ OCCASION.
_____	☐1 38	☐1 39	☐1 40
_____	☐2	☐2	☐2
_____	☐3	☐3	☐3
_____	☐4	☐4	☐4
_____	☐5	☐5	☐5
_____	☐6	☐6	☐6
_____	☐7	☐7	☐7

23. If you had free choice in the matter, how much time would you give to the following?

	MORE THAN NOW	SAME AMOUNT	LESS THAN NOW	
Classroom instruction	☐1	☐2	☐3	41
Your own graduate education	☐1	☐2	☐3	42
Research or professional writing	☐1	☐2	☐3	43
Administrative activities	☐1	☐2	☐3	44
Professional association work	☐1	☐2	☐3	45
Community service	☐1	☐2	☐3	46
Personal affairs	☐1	☐2	☐3	47
Student interaction outside class	☐1	☐2	☐3	48
Conferring with colleagues	☐1	☐2	☐3	49
Reading student papers or tests	☐1	☐2	☐3	50
Planning instruction	☐1	☐2	☐3	51
Presenting recitals or lectures outside of class	☐1	☐2	☐3	52

24. On your most recent working day how many hours did you spend in:

a. Classroom instruction _____ Hrs. 53-54
b. Your own graduate education _____ Hrs. 55-56
c. Research or professional writing _____ Hrs. 57-58
d. Administrative activities (including committee work) _____ Hrs. 59-60
e. Professional association work _____ Hrs. 61-62
f. Community service _____ Hrs. 63-64
g. Personal affairs _____ Hrs. 65-66
h. Student interaction outside class _____ Hrs. 67-68
i. Informal interaction with colleagues _____ Hrs. 69-70
j. Reading student papers or tests _____ Hrs. 71-72
k. Planning instruction _____ Hrs. 73-74

11 - 3

25a. Would you like to take steps toward professional development in the next five years?

YES ☐1   NO, I'VE GONE AS FAR AS I CAN ☐2   12

(If "Yes"):

25b. Which one of the following most appeals to you? (CHECK ONE)   13

ENROLL IN COURSES IN A UNIV. ☐1

GET A PH.D. OR ED.D. ☐2

GET A DOCTOR OF ARTS DEGREE ☐3

GET A MASTER'S DEGREE ☐4

ENROLL IN IN SERVICE COURSES AT YOUR COLLEGE ☐5

OTHER (Specify) _____ ☐

26. If you had a free summer, what would you do with it?

14-15

27. What type of training would you seek before teaching if you were to begin all over again?   16-17

28. Five years from now (1980) you might be considering the following positions. How attractive do they appear to you at this time?

		VERY ATTRACTIVE	SOMEWHAT ATTRACTIVE	UN- ATTRACTIVE	
a.	A faculty position at a four-year college or university	☐1	☐2	☐3	18
b.	A faculty position at another community or junior college	☐1	☐2	☐3	19
c.	An administrative position in a community or junior college	☐1	☐2	☐3	20
d.	A position in a professional association	☐1	☐2	☐3	21
e.	A school outside the United States	☐1	☐2	☐3	22
f.	Any position but this college	☐1	☐2	☐3	23
g.	A non-teaching, non-academic position	☐1	☐2	☐3	24
h.	I would be doing what I'm doing now	☐1	☐2	☐3	25
i.	I have no idea.	☐1	☐2	☐3	26

29. What has been your affiliation with professional organizations in the past three years?

	MEMBER 27-28	ATTENDED A REGIONAL OR NATIONAL MEETING 29-30	PRESENTED A PAPER 31-32
American Association of University Professors	☐1	☐1	☐1
American Federation of Teachers (or affiliate)	☐2	☐2	☐2
National Education Association (or affiliate)	☐3	☐3	☐3
Other national or regional organizations in your subject area (e.g., American Historical Association, National Council of Teachers of English, American Council on Teaching of Foreign Languages) (Please specify):			
_____	☐1	☐1	☐1
_____	☐2	☐2	☐2
_____	☐3	☐3	☐3

30. How would you rate the qualities that students should gain from a two-year college education?

		VERY IMPORTANT	LESS IMPORTANT	
a.	Knowledge and skill directly applicable to their careers	☐1	☐2	33
b.	An understanding and mastery of some academic discipline	☐1	☐2	34
c.	Preparation for further formal education	☐1	☐2	35
d.	Self-knowledge and a personal identity	☐1	☐2	36
e.	Aesthetic awareness	☐1	☐2	37
f.	Knowledge of and interest in community and world problems	☐1	☐2	38

Many of the questions in the following section pertain particularly to humanities education. Even if you are not an instructor in the humanities, we are very much interested in your opinions and we would like your responses to these items. For purposes of this study, the humanities includes the following subject areas separately or in combination:

aesthetics	jurisprudence
art history or appreciation	linguistics
comparative religion	literary criticism
cultural anthropology	literature
cultural geography	music history or appreciation
English	philosophy, ethics, logic
foreign languages	political science
history	theater history or appreciation

31.   How many humanities courses do you think students in two-year occupational programs should be required to take?

NONE ☐1   ONE ☐2   TWO ☐3   THREE ☐4   FOUR   ☐5   FIVE ☐6   SIX OR MORE ☐7   NO OPINION ☐8   39

32.   The humanities can be offered through other than course-related presentation. Do you think there are too few, sufficient, or too many of these activities open to students at your college?

		TOO FEW	SUFFICIENT	TOO MANY	DON'T KNOW	
a.	Colloquiums and seminars	☐1	☐2	☐3	☐4	40
b.	Lectures	☐1	☐2	☐3	☐4	41
c.	Exhibits	☐1	☐2	☐3	☐4	42
d.	Concerts and recitals	☐1	☐2	☐3	☐4	43
e.	Films	☐1	☐2	☐3	☐4	44

33.   How do you experience the humanities other than through your teaching?

45-46

34.   What changes in humanities instruction have taken place at your college in the past seven years?

47-48

35.   What changes would you like to see effected?

49-50

36.   How do you feel about the following?

	STRONGLY AGREE	SOMEWHAT AGREE	DON'T KNOW OR NO OPINION	SOMEWHAT DISAGREE	STRONGLY DISAGREE	
a. Overall, this institution's administration is creative and effective	☐1	☐2	☐3	☐4	☐5	51
b. This college should be actively engaged in community services	☐1	☐2	☐3	☐4	☐5	52
c. Most faculty members should take some type of academic course work or engage in a creative activity (e.g., writing a book) at least every three years	☐1	☐2	☐3	☐4	☐5	53
d. Teaching the humanities to students in occupational and remedial programs is different from teaching transfer students	☐1	☐2	☐3	☐4	☐5	54
e. I feel considerable personal strain in my commitments to different aspects of my job	☐1	☐2	☐3	☐4	☐5	55
f. It is as important for a person to experience his emotions and feelings as it is to develop his intellectual or cognitive skills	☐1	☐2	☐3	☐4	☐5	56
g. All too often the present is filled with unhappiness. It's only the future that counts.	☐1	☐2	☐3	☐4	☐5	57
h. Collective bargaining by faculty members has a definite place in a community college	☐1	☐2	☐3	☐4	☐5	58
i. I believe that if I work hard, things will work out for me	☐1	☐2	☐3	☐4	☐5	59
j. Faculty members in all kinds of higher education institutions should engage in a process of self-evaluation	☐1	☐2	☐3	☐4	☐5	60
k. Career education and occupational training should be the major emphasis in today's community college	☐1	☐2	☐3	☐4	☐5	61
l. Most humanities instructors are well prepared to teach	☐1	☐2	☐3	☐4	☐5	62
m. Growth is a never ending process and should be a continuous quest	☐1	☐2	☐3	☐4	☐5	63
n. Exciting developments are taking place in the humanities	☐1	☐2	☐3	☐4	☐5	64
o. The humanities are being diminished in importance in the community college	☐1	☐2	☐3	☐4	☐5	65
p. Satisfactory opportunities for inservice training are not available at this college	☐1	☐2	☐3	☐4	☐5	66

	STRONGLY AGREE	SOMEWHAT AGREE	DON'T KNOW OR NO OPINION	SOMEWHAT DISAGREE	STRONGLY DISAGREE	
q. As a child I felt especially proud of my mother, father, or other member of my family	☐1	☐2	☐3	☐4	☐5	67
r. Teaching effectiveness should be the primary basis for faculty promotion	☐1	☐2	☐3	☐4	☐5	68
s. Faculty promotions should be based in part on formal student evaluations of their teachers	☐1	☐2	☐3	☐4	☐5	69
t. Faculty should engage in more inter-disciplinary courses	☐1	☐2	☐3	☐4	☐5	70
u. I would like to have closer contacts with university faculty members who teach the same course I teach	☐1	☐2	☐3	☐4	☐5	71
v. The administration of my department is not very democratic	☐1	☐2	☐3	☐4	☐5	72
w. I prefer to teach small classes	☐1	☐2	☐3	☐4	☐5	73
y. Claims of discriminatory practices against women and minority students in higher education have been greatly exaggerated	☐1	☐2	☐3	☐4	☐5	74
y. I tend to pattern my teaching after my own college or university courses	☐1	☐2	☐3	☐4	☐5	75
z. There should be preferential hiring for women and/or minority faculty at this institution	☐1	☐2	☐3	☐4	☐5	11 - 4 / 12
aa. If I had a chance to retrace my steps, I would not choose an academic life	☐1	☐2	☐3	☐4	☐5	13
bb. Knowledge in my field is expanding so fast that I need further training in order to keep up	☐1	☐2	☐3	☐4	☐5	14
cc. Compared with most people of my age in my field who have had comparable training, I have been more successful	☐1	☐2	☐3	☐4	☐5	15
dd. Students should not have representation on the governing boards of colleges and universities	☐1	☐2	☐3	☐4	☐5	16
ee. Most of the important ideas about the humanities emanate from the university	☐1	☐2	☐3	☐4	☐5	17
ff. The same humanities courses should be given to humanities and non-humanities students (e.g., occupational students, science majors)	☐1	☐2	☐3	☐4	☐5	18
gg. Time hangs heavy on my hands when I am not teaching or acting as a college administrator	☐1	☐2	☐3	☐4	☐5	19
hh. The humanities curriculum in my college should be modified	☐1	☐2	☐3	☐4	☐5	20

37. People often feel differently with different groups and in different situations.

Which figure or figures in the boxes below best describe how you see yourself in relation to the different groups listed? (You may choose the same figure or different figures for your responses. Please mark one box in each row.)

	FIG. A	FIG. B	FIG. C	FIG. D	FIG. E	FIG. F	
Other instructors in my field	☐ 1	☐ 2	☐ 3	☐ 4	☐ 5	☐ 6	21
Most instructors at this school	☐ 1	☐ 2	☐ 3	☐ 4	☐ 5	☐ 6	22
My family	☐ 1	☐ 2	☐ 3	☐ 4	☐ 5	☐ 6	23
My group of friends	☐ 1	☐ 2	☐ 3	☐ 4	☐ 5	☐ 6	24
Teacher organizations	☐ 1	☐ 2	☐ 3	☐ 4	☐ 5	☐ 6	25
My students	☐ 1	☐ 2	☐ 3	☐ 4	☐ 5	☐ 6	26
College administrators	☐ 1	☐ 2	☐ 3	☐ 4	☐ 5	☐ 6	27

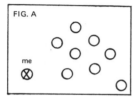

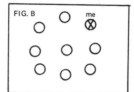

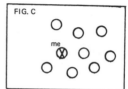

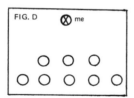

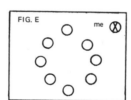

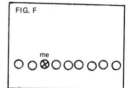

38. Below is a list of 18 values* arranged in alphabetical order. We are interested in finding out the relative importance of these values to <u>you.</u> Study the list carefully and pick out the one value which is the most important for you. Place a <u>1</u> on the blank line to the left of this value and cross it off your list. Look at the remaining 17 values; which is <u>second</u> most important for you? Place a 2 next to this value and cross it off your list. Look at the remaining 16 values and rank them in order of importance. The value which is <u>least</u> important should be ranked 18th.

_____	A COMFORTABLE LIFE (a prosperous life)	28-29
_____	EQUALITY (brotherhood, equal opportunity for all)	30-31
_____	AN EXCITING LIFE (a stimulating, active life)	32-33
_____	FAMILY SECURITY (taking care of loved ones)	34-35
_____	FREEDOM (independence, free choice)	36-37
_____	HAPPINESS (contentedness)	38-39
_____	INNER HARMONY (freedom from inner conflict)	40-41
_____	MATURE LOVE (sexual and spiritual intimacy)	42-43
_____	NATIONAL SECURITY (protection from attack)	44-45
_____	PLEASURE (an enjoyable, leisurely life)	46-47
_____	SALVATION (saved, eternal life)	48-49
_____	SELF-RESPECT (self-esteem)	50-51
_____	A SENSE OF ACCOMPLISHMENT (lasting contribution)	52-53
_____	SOCIAL RECOGNITION (respect, admiration)	54-55
_____	TRUE FRIENDSHIP (close companionship)	56-57
_____	WISDOM (a mature understanding of life)	58-59
_____	A WORLD AT PEACE (free of war and conflict)	60-61
_____	A WORLD OF BEAUTY (beauty of nature and the arts)	62-63

*Rokeach Terminal Values Scale

IMPORTANT INSTRUCTIONS

Thank you for taking the time to complete this questionnaire. To ensure your confidentiality we have provided you with two envelopes. Please seal the completed questionnaire in the small envelope marked "CONFIDENTIAL." Place this in the larger envelope which is addressed to the project facilitator on your campus and return it to him or her.

After collecting all the forms from your colleagues, the facilitator will remove the outer envelopes and discard them, returning to the Center only your sealed confidential survey forms.

We appreciate your prompt attention and participation in this important educational survey.

Alabama
James Faulkner
LurleenWallace

Arizona
Arizona Western
Mesa
Pima

Arkansas
Arkansas State

California
American River
Barstow
Butte
Citrus
College of the Desert
De Anza
Fresno
Hartnell
Humphreys
Lassen
Mendocino
Mt. San Jacinto
Pierce
Saddleback
San Diego Mesa
San Mateo
Santa Rosa

Colorado
Denver
Morgan

Connecticut
Greater Hartford
Middlesex
Mitchell
Quinebaug Valley

Delaware
Delaware Technical
Goldey Beacom

Florida
Brevard
Indian River
Miami-Dade
Palm Beach
St. Petersburg
Valencia

Georgia
Floyd
Middle Georgia

Hawaii
Kauai

Illinois
Central YMCA
Danville
Lincoln Land
Oakton
Southwest
Waubonsee

Iowa
Clinton
Iowa Lakes
Marshalltown
Mt. St. Claire
Southeastern

Kansas
Barton
Central
Coffeyville
Hesston

167

Kentucky
Southeast

Maine
University of Maine/Augusta

Maryland
Cecil
Hagerstown
Harford
Howard

Massachusetts
Bay Patch
Bunker Hill
Garland
Greenfield
Leicester
Mt. Wachusett
Roxbury
Wentworth

Michigan
Delta
Monroe County
Oakland/Auburn
Suomi

Minnesota
Austin
North Hennepin
University of Minnesota/Waseca

Mississippi
Jefferson Davis
Mary Holmes
Itawamba
Southwest Mississippi
Wood

Missouri
St. Paul's
Trenton

Nebraska
Metro Technical
Platte

Nevada
Clark County

New Hampshire
New Hampshire/Claremont
White Plains

New Jersey
Atlantic
Middlesex

New Mexico
University of New Mexico/Gallup

New York
Fashion Technical
Harriman
Hudson Valley
Mohawk Valley
North Country
Staten Island

North Carolina
Chowan
Coastal Carolina
Edgecombe Technical
Lenoir
Mt. Olive
Wake Technical
Wingate

Ohio
Belmont Technical
Cuyahoga Eastern
Lorain
Ohio University/Portsmouth
Ohio University/Belmont
Sinclair
University of Toledo Technical

Oklahoma
Connors State
Northern Oklahoma
South Oklahoma City
St. Gregorys

Oregon
Chemeketa
Mt. Hood
Treasure Valley

Pennsylvania
Allegheny County
Delaware County
Harcum
Keystone
Northampton
Northeast Christian

South Carolina
Greenville Technical
Lancaster, University of South
  Carolina

South Dakota
Presentation

Tennessee
Jackson State
Martin
Morristown

Texas
Angelina
Cooke County
Lamar
Western Texas

Utah
Utah Technical

Vermont
Champlain
Vermont College

Virginia
Central Virginia
Northern Virginia
J.S. Reynolds
Southern Seminary
Tidewater
Wytheville

Washington
Columbia Basin
Green River
Peninsula
South Seattle
Spokane

West Virginia
West Virginia Northern

Wisconsin
District One Technical
Fox Valley
Lakeshore
Milwaukee Area Technical
University Center System/Sheboygan

Wyoming
Casper

INDEX

administrators, 28
advisory committees, 114, 115
affirmative action, 3, 4, 5, 118
age of college, 30, 50–51, 75
age of faculty, 27, 35, 53, 72, 75, 87
Alabama, 69
American Association of Community and
    Junior Colleges, 4, 11, 56, 93
American Association for Higher Education,
    6
American Association of University Pro-
    fessors, 6
American Council on Education, 5, 9, 13,
    20, 21, 52, 74
American Federation of Teachers, 6
anthropology, 42
anthropology instructors, 53, 116
art instructors, 59, 116; and "concern for
    students," 48; and "research ori-
    entation," 53
associate degrees, 99
attitudes and values, 14, 18–24
automotive technology instructors, 114,
    116

Barrett, T.C., 26
Bayer, A.E. 5, 7, 9, 52, 74
Benewitz, M.C., 6
biology instructors, 114
Bloom, M., Ralph, N., and Freedman,
    M., 23
books in home, 54
Brawer, F.B., 16, 22, 30, 33, 38
Bresler, J.B., 53
Brown, J.L., 2, 4
Brown, J.S., and Shukraft, R.C., 31
Bushnell, D.S., 5, 9, 19

California, 2, 4, 5, 13, 22, 24, 25, 38, 56,
    57, 59, 93, 94
California Education Code, 58
career education, 20
career programs, 1
Carnegie-Mellon University, 78, 121
Carnegie Commission on Higher Education,
    19, 25
Cartter, A.M., and Salter, M.M., 74

Center for the Study of Community Col-
    leges, 4, 6, 10
Champion, D., and Sear, A.M., 9
chairpersons, 10, 17, 75, 83, 85, 87; and
    "concern for students," 48; and
    "curriculum and instruction," 44;
    and "functional potential," 35; and
    "research orientation," 54; and
    "satisfaction," 27
change of environment, 31
Chicago City-wide Institute, 2
classics instructors, 116
clinical professors, 77, 121
Coastline Community College, 2
Cohen, A.M., 26, 52
Cohen, A.M., and Associates, 26
Cohen, A.M., and Brawer, F.B., 30, 33, 52,
    70
collective bargaining, 3, 6, 7, 19, 111 (see
    also, unionization)
College Composition and Communication,
    53
college presidents, 10, 11
colleges: regional differences, 59–60, 76;
    size, 104; survey sample, 10, 11,
    12–13
colleges without walls, 2, 94
community-based education, 2, 103, 116
*Community College Social Science
    Quarterly*, 54
Community College of Vermont, 2
community services, 98, 117
comprehensive colleges, 31, 50
"concern for students," 15, 44, 51; art
    instructors, 49; of chairpersons, 48;
    and "concern with humanities,"
    51, 87–88; and "curriculum and
    instruction," 44, 51; doctoral de-
    grees, 48; foreign language instruc-
    tors, 48; and "functional potential,"
    38, 51; liberal arts instructors, 48;
    music instructors, 48; philosophy
    instructors, 48; "preference for
    further preparation," 51, 73; profes-
    sional associations, 48; professional
    development, 48; "research orienta-
    tion," 51, 55; and "satisfaction,"

170

ARTHUR M. COHEN is a Professor in Higher Education at the University of California, Los Angeles, where he has been since 1964. He is the founding director of the ERIC Clearinghouse for Junior Colleges, a nationwide information retrieval, analysis, and dissemination center located at UCLA, and president of the Center for the Study of Community Colleges, in Los Angeles.

Dr. Cohen has lectured, conducted research studies, and written extensively about two-year colleges. His articles have appeared in 20 different professional journals, and he is editor-in chief of *New Directions for Community Colleges*. His books include *Dateline '79: Heretical Concepts for the Community Colleges* (1969); and, with his associates, he has written *A Constant Variable: The New Perspectives on the Community College* (1971), *Confronting Identity: The Community College Instructor* (1972), and *College Responses to Community Demands* (1975).

Dr. Cohen's undergraduate and master's degree preparation was in History at the University of Miami. His doctorate in Higher Education was obtained at The Florida State University.

FLORENCE B. BRAWER is Research Director of the Center for the Study of Community Colleges, lecturer in Higher Education at UCLA, and research educationist at the ERIC Clearinghouse for Junior Colleges at UCLA. She has been a counselor and psychometrist in both a junior college and a university.

Brawer has published in the areas of psychology and education. Her articles have appeared in *Journal of Analytic Psychology*, *Journal of Personality Assessment*, *Journal of Teacher Education*, and numerous other journals. Her books include *New Perspectives on Personality Development in College Students* (1973), *Developments in the Rorschach Technique, Vol. III* (1970), and several others done in association with Arthur M. Cohen.

She holds a B.A. from the University of Michigan and an M.A. and an Ed.D. from the University of California, Los Angeles.

COLLEGE AS A TRAINING GROUND FOR JOBS
Lewis C. Solmon
Ann S. Bisconti
Nancy L. Ochsner

A DEGREE OF DIFFERENCE: The Open University of the United Kingdom
Naomi E. McIntosh,
with Judith A. Calder
Betty Swift

MINORITIES IN U.S. INSTITUTIONS OF HIGHER EDUCATION
Frank Brown
Madelon D. Stent